Shortcut to Heaven

Robert Bush

Copyright © 2011 by Robert Bush

Shortcut to Heaven
by Robert Bush

Printed in the United States of America

ISBN 9781612159140

All rights reserved solely by the author. The author guarantees all contents are original and do not infringe upon the legal rights of any other person or work. No part of this book may be reproduced in any form without the permission of the author. The views expressed in this book are not necessarily those of the publisher.

Unless otherwise indicated, Bible quotations are taken from The HOLY BIBLE, NEW INTERNATIONAL VERSION®. Copyright © 1973, 1978, 1984 by International Bible Society. Used by permission of Zondervan Publishing House.

The "NIV" and "New International Version" trademarks are registered in the United States Patent and Trademark Office by International Bible Society. Use of either trademark requires the permission of the International Bible Society.

www.xulonpress.com

Dedicated to

*F*irst and foremost, to my Lord and Savior, Jesus Christ, who stuck with me even though I was not worthy. When those around me need a helping hand and positive encouragement, I hope I am able to exemplify Him through my actions. I am truly humbled by what you have done for me…thank you for not giving up on me:

> *What can I possibly do to repay you? There is no way I can even come close, but I do promise to refocus my energy and passion to go down the path that you have laid before me. This book is simply a small way of saying "thank you" to the one who died for me, for without Him, I would be nothing. I hope and pray that the words in this book touch the hearts of those who read them. Personal encouragement and strength, for all of my readers, is what I will pray for daily.*

To My Wife, for she is the one who has made me whole, the one who has supported me in everything I have done. I love you with all my heart and soul. Thank you for sticking by my side regarding this book and for encouraging me along the way:

My mind races with thoughts that seem to engulf my every move, yet through it all, I feel a peace that can only be explained by the love and sacrifice of our Lord and Savior...Jesus Christ. I search through the empty faces of the crowd for a sign of light, a glimmer of hope, only to find a world self-indulged on mindless iniquities and thoughts that have no bearing on why we are here. My memory is shallow, yet through it all; you push and push until somehow those happy thoughts make their way to the crevasse of my soul. And just as discouragement begins to seep into my mind like a blood-thirsty predator that threatens my new heart, you are able to pull me through my moment of confusion and despair. I cannot see Jesus, but I know He lives, because I see the remnants of His special sparkle in you. So...as I close my eyes, I search. I search that empty crowd for you because you are my glimmer of hope, my inspiration, my love, my life, and my best friend. And just as my eyes begin to open; you slowly disappear, so I close them even tighter than before. As I close them, your smile consumes me and peace finds a resting place in my soul. I do not want to open them again because I am afraid you will go away, and I will be faced with a world that only wants to harden my heart and pull me into the bowels of untimely death. Instead, just when I feel like my life is unraveling and hopelessness begins to burrow its way in, I open my eyes and you are there, even more beautiful than in my dreams. Through it all, I realize the essence of life is really quite simple. In a world full of uncertainty, negativity, and doubt, you have made it very clear. I am here right now surviving because of you. For you bring me hope, faith, and love, and somehow I pull myself from the darkness that continually rests on the other side of the door. The stench of the enemy awaits, but he cannot enter because you are with me. I hold you tight praying you will never go away. You squeeze me back, and my body becomes energized with a passion for love, life, and my Lord and Savior. And for that I am grateful…I love you, honey. Thank you for finding me just when I needed you the most.

To Our Daughters, for they have taught me so much:

Your love for the Lord and each other has made me realize just how blessed I am to be your father. Can your daughters actually be your heroes...the answer is quite simply yes! Thank you for teaching me what it means to truly love someone, regardless of color, race, or economic status. Your willingness to reach out to those in need has made me proud beyond words, and I know both of you are going to make an incredible difference in this world. To know that our family will be together in heaven forever has given me an incredible peace, and I will always be grateful for your smiles and your love. May the Lord continue to bless you and keep you safe; stay focused and diligent in Him. Remember...life is all about how you finish the race. You will undoubtedly finish it with Him. And for that, I have the ultimate peace, for I know that I will also be waiting there for you when you arrive.

To My Parents, for they have taught me the importance of hard work, perseverance, and humility:

Thank you, Mom and Dad, for always being there for me. Your constant words of encouragement can still be heard, as I think back at all the things you have done for me. I am especially grateful for your encouragement regarding this book. You have allowed me to water a dream and watch it grow. Without your constant support and love, I would be nothing. You have made me a better husband and father because I have learned from you. The greatest gift you ever gave me was your continual encouragement and support. You always made me believe that I could be anyone I wanted to be...thank you!

To My Fellow Brothers and Sisters in Christ who sit on the School Board, for without your prayers, my journey could not have been possible:

Your love for the Lord is incredible. I am in awe of you every time we are together. I am truly humbled by your love of Jesus, as everything you do is about Him. I truly know what it means to pray to God regarding everything we do, with a firm belief that He is in control. I see you pray for our school, our teachers, and our kids every day, and I know God is watching with tears in His eyes. Being around you has made me stronger in my faith, and this is the greatest gift you could have ever given me.

To All the Parents and Siblings of Sick Children, who face incredible tests of faith each and every day:

These families are quickly thrown into the confines of their own worst nightmare, as they are expected to show compassion, empathy, strength, and most of all, faith at all times…an impossible task at best. In a matter of seconds, lives can be torn to shreds with an unanticipated phone call that will bring even the strongest non-believers to their knees praying for help. You see…we realize early on in life that nobody is immune to these life-changing events. Unanticipated tragedies that can literally take and transform a person from one who has denied the existence of God, to one who realizes that everything we do should be for Him. Through the course of these surreal experiences, we find ourselves continually asking the question, "Why is this happening to my little boy or my little girl?" Soon, we realize that the real question we should be asking is, "What can I do to further my faith and draw others to Him, even though I feel too weak to go on?" This does not seem realistic, as our bodies of flesh continually revert back to finger-pointing and relentless thoughts of guilt that consume our every move. Bitterness is our own worst enemy, yet he constantly attacks us, hoping for a moment of weakness so he can infiltrate our minds. We must find a way to choose a path of faith and hope, and rise above the enemy's attempt to discourage us and bring us down. On a personal level, we found this out ourselves back in July of 2005...and this is why I have now devoted my life to the message I have captured in this book.

CONTENTS

Dedication v
Introduction xv
Closing Remarks 177

Chapter 1 Three Taps/**Suffering** 25

Chapter 2 His Father's Eyes/**Humility** 38

Chapter 3 The Last One Chosen/**Seeds of Strength** 46

Chapter 4 Back of Mind/**Forgiveness** 60

Chapter 5 Eyes of Blue/**Grace** 80

Chapter 6	Best Friends Forever/**Courage**	98
Chapter 7	Steam from a Grate/**Faith**	115
Chapter 8	Till Death Do Us Part/**Peace**	133
Chapter 9	The Blue Ribbon Prize/**Thankfulness**	149
Chapter 10	My Last Day/**Love**	160

Introduction...
why I wrote this book

Life was perfect for our family, and nothing could possibly derail me from the career that had consumed nearly every waking moment of my life for the past 22 years...at least, I didn't think anything could ever get in the way. My priorities revolved around three meaningless metrics, better known in my business world as revenue growth, profit margin, and cash flow. Although I had been personally saved since October of 1997, my faith had never been truly tested until the summer of 2005. This was the absolute turning point in my life, when I realized just how powerful and awesome God was...how He was the one who was in control of my life, __not me__. Everything was going along very smoothly for our family, but this would all change in the blink of an eye. This was when I got the phone call that changed everything...our lives were literally turned upside down before we knew what hit us. I was absolutely powerless in a matter of seconds. I am sure each of you can relate to something that has happened in your own personal life where you felt this same sense of vulnerability, when you found out just how weak you really are…when you felt like it was impossible to go on? So, what in the world are we supposed to do in this moment of truth, when our personal walls of perceived security are crashing in on us? This is when all of us need to be ready to totally trust in God, not just a little, but with everything we have inside us. Simply put… we **_cannot_** face these challenges alone! All of a sudden, my sales organization's revenue number didn't mean anything to me. Priorities were completely flipped upside down, with my little girl's survival replacing everything else in my life. My head was pounding in disbelief, and the fear that consumed my every thought was spinning out of control. Although I knew I wasn't supposed to let this happen to me, I couldn't stop from thinking about what "may" happen from this point forward. I remember lying on the bed with my head buried in my hands, crying uncontrollably after I hung up the phone. How could this be happening to us? Wasn't it always supposed to be someone else who got the call? Trust me when I say this…there will be a time for each of us, when it is **_not_** the other guy or gal. At some point in time, all of us will go through a life-changing event that rocks our world. So... what are we going to do when this happens? What are we supposed to do in order to weather the storm and rise above the negativity that constantly surrounds us in this world? Why do we all seem to need that dreaded phone call in order to establish the true priorities in our life? When are we all going to realize that our focus should always be on Him, no matter what the circumstance? Remember...it is much easier to praise God when things are going well; however, we must also praise Him and trust Him when we are going through the valleys in our lives as well. This faith walk will make us stronger and ultimately prepare us for what He has in store for us at the next stop...because heaven will be awesome!

I have prayed about, and written this book, with one critical objective in mind: I want you to know that there is, in fact, a **_shortcut to heaven_**, an extremely easy path that everyone needs to walk down today. However, understanding how to get to heaven is really the easiest part of this message! All of us must realize that this is just the beginning regarding our own personal journey. Once we understand how to get to heaven, we now become a primary target of the enemy, and our minds must be stronger than ever! Becoming a Christian is definitely the first step we must take in our journey and is, in fact, the easiest segment of our walk. However, living the life of a Christian can be a totally different story. *Shortcut to Heaven* is **not** just another self-help book with motivational excerpts that you will read and forget in the same day. When I started to think about how I could have the greatest positive impact on my readers, I prayed about what vehicle of delivery would be best…and it became obvious to me that I needed to establish this encouragement through scenarios that everyone can relate to on a daily basis. This book contains ten separate stories, each depicting a specific message that is tied to Scripture. Jesus was the master of teaching through parables, as evidenced in the Bible. *Shortcut to Heaven* is designed to focus on key Christian principles, but bring them to life through these stories that make us think about our own trials and tribulations as well. Each of the ten stories you read will reflect a specific passage of encouragement that will allow you to persevere through the difficult times you may be facing. You will find through the characters in this book that your problems can be worked out, and that you are not alone in your fight for inner peace. At the end of the day, this is our ultimate goal…the peace of the Lord. But…how in the world do we get there? All of us have friends who are wealthy and seem to have everything in their lives; however, their outward appearance does not truly reflect the turmoil they are feeling on the inside. This is because their definition of inner peace resonates on worldly views, without a true focus on God. On the other hand, we have all met individuals who seem to have nothing when it comes to worldly things, but man, do they have inner peace! They carry themselves with an incredible level of confidence that has nothing at all to do with humanly possessions. It has to do with their relationship with God. They know where they are going when they die, and they know what their purpose on earth is before they get there! Defining the purpose God has for us, and living it out as well each and every day, is critical regarding our personal attainment of true peace. We all strive for this inner state of mind, body, and soul...the feeling that cannot be described through words, but can only be attained as we get closer to God. This book will not only help you find the shortcut to heaven, because there truly is a straight and narrow path, but it will help you fight through the attacks you will be facing once you start down this incredible journey. You see...one of the biggest mistakes we make as Christians is we fall into the trap of believing that our work is done once a commitment to the Lord is made. No way! This is where we need to be more focused than ever on the path we have taken...the path that will undoubtedly be lined with land mines disguised as illusions, temptations, and potential pitfalls of life-changing transgressions. We need to avoid these illusions and continually keep our focus on Him…at all times!

Every one of us will have a significant event at some point in time that will force us to look at our own life differently. Our inner self will be exposed, and we will need to make sure we address those areas of our soul that are corrupt. How we respond to this event can ultimately shape the direction we take as men and women. More often than not, these events convince us that God is in absolute control of our lives. **_We operate under His time line, not ours_**. This can impose a number of problems on those of us who are inherently impatient and also operate under the false assumption that we are in control. I found this out firsthand, which made me clearly understand that I needed to write this book. It made me realize that there are millions of others out there just like me who are going through difficult times and need real-life encouragement…with a direct correlation to Scripture. Not an exercise program, an updated diet, or a meaningless fad of some kind. It needs to be focused on God, as this is where our true encouragement lies…

My wake-up call came during the summer of 2005. Our daughter, who was 11 years old at the time, was inflicted with a tumor that had embedded itself into her jaw. The tumor extended from just below her left eye, down along her jaw, and ultimately wrapped itself around her beautiful chin. However, none of us had any idea this was happening, as we continued to fall in love with her infectious smile each and every day. Her jawbone was soon engulfed by the rapid expansion of this unsuspected enemy, as it grew into the size of a tennis ball nearly overnight. Our lives went on day by day, without any realization that this tumor had taken on the impersonation of real bone. Had it not been for a routine dental exam, we would have never found this tumor. Since our daughter was asymptomatic at the time with no pain whatsoever, we had no idea how our lives would soon be turned upside down when the tumor finally reared its ugly head. One phone call, one diagnosis…would change our lives forever. This event was the impetus behind the book you are about to read. I realized that within seconds, our lives would never be the same. Daily challenges that we were accustomed to soon became irrelevant, as life's true priorities took the place of those things that we thought were important. Never again would we look at life the same way. We realized that our misfortune was something thousands of families go through every day. I remember when our daughter came out of her five-hour surgery, and I had finally gathered up enough strength to go down and get a bite to eat in the cafeteria at Children's Hospital. We had only been in the hospital a couple of days, but we were already emotionally exhausted. I remember going through the food line and looking over at a family that was sitting at a table, not far from where I was standing. Mom and Dad were feeding their little boy, who was sitting next to them in a small booster seat. He had no hair and his body looked frail and almost grey in color. I remember thinking about how tired I was and wondering how those parents were coping at such an incredibly difficult time. They looked exhausted, but they continued to feed their little guy, somehow gathering up enough strength for a momentary smile now and then. I looked around the cafeteria and there were multiple groups of parents with their sick children dispersed everywhere, all trying to muster up enough strength to go on. We were all battling through the same questions of uncertainty that day…all of us wishing we were the ones who were sick, rather than our kids. Is there anything worse than a terminally ill child? I don't think so. I had no idea there were so many sick children in this country, and so many parents struggling with feelings of helplessness, disbelief, anger, and self-pity…just like we were.

I have been working on this book for a number of years. When our daughter was sick, I turned to a number of great books with the hope that one of them would somehow relate to what I was going through. While all of them were terrific self-help motivational books, I was unable to connect with any of them during my time of need. My problems were different, and I needed more. This is when I realized that there were many others out there in a position just like me, trying to get away and read something that was truly relevant. I needed to find the words that somehow reflected the way I was feeling at the time. I started to pray and really trust God that He would give me a vision as to how I could, in fact, make a difference through the words He had placed in my soul. It worked! My passion to make a difference through this book, and others to follow, is at an all-time high.

I hope and pray that *Shortcut to Heaven* provides you with limitless encouragement and the belief that you can get through anything in this world with God. He knows our limitations for He created each and every one of us. He will never give us more than we can handle...truly believing this is critical to our daily survival. Our ability to put the pieces of our own personal wall back together again when things are falling apart will depend on one critical factor...our ability to focus on Him, no matter what the circumstance. There is a shortcut to heaven; however, that's just the first step. Once you decide to go down this path, you will undoubtedly become a marked man or woman. Why is this? Because you are furthering the kingdom of God...something the enemy hates! This book is designed to keep you on that path, recognizing that there will, in fact, be strong challenges along the way. However, if we focus on Him and stick together, we will all be in heaven some day…and there is plenty of room for everyone. *Shortcut to Heaven* is all about the path and the journey…encouragement for all, no matter where you are in your own personal walk.

Enjoy and May God Bless Each of You Always…

Chapter One

"Three Taps"

Suffering…1 Peter 3:17-18
"It is better, if it is God's will, to suffer for doing good than for doing evil. For Christ died for sins once for all, the righteous for the unrighteous, to bring you to God. He was put to death in the body but made alive by the Spirit."

The man entered the room and breathed an extended sigh of relief. He had finally made it back to the hotel after a long day of meetings and an evening workshop with customers. Orlando had been very good to him that day, as business was really starting to pick up. He couldn't help but remember the way it was just last year. He took off his coat and closed the door behind him. The anticipation of calling his family and getting caught up on their day's activities was his only concern right now. As good as the day had been, the best part was yet to come. Oh, how the man looked forward to the calls back home to his wife and two young daughters. Although they were growing up quickly, he was still "Daddy" in their eyes, and they told him so every day. Oh, how he dreaded the days that would slowly creep into his life…when Daddy would be replaced with Dad. Hopefully, those days would never come. As he turned to set his jacket on the chair next to the bed, he noticed the telephone light was blinking off and on. He dialed the operator and asked for his messages. "Your wife has been trying to reach you," said the night manager. "She wants you to give her a call." The man reached down and checked his cell phone…no messages. That was just like her…she didn't want to call him during the meeting, so she rang his room instead. He smiled, as he began to take off his white shirt and tie. He dialed the number and waited for her voice. "Hello," she said. "Is everything ok?" the man said, with uneasy trepidation. Silence was the answer he received…he wasn't ready for the news that was about to come. He could hear her sobbing gently into the telephone, and he knew his life would never be the same. The same could be said for his family as well…

"It's ok, sweetheart. I am here now so just take your time and tell me what's going on. Are you and the girls ok…was there an accident?" asked the man, as his heart began to race uncontrollably. "No...we are doing just fine, but I need to tell you about something that happened today." The man breathed a momentary sigh of relief. He braced himself for the news. "So, what is it, honey?" he asked, as he sat back in his chair. "The girls and I went to the dentist today for our check-up. This was our last visit before the move, so I wanted to make sure we said good-bye to everyone, and that everything was ok before we transferred our records. As I was getting ready to leave, John pulled me aside and told me he needed to speak with me about the X-rays that were just run. He told me he didn't like what he saw...and I could feel myself start to tremble. I just didn't know what to say." The man could hear his wife begin to sob once again...being away and out of town tonight made it even more difficult. "So, what did he say, honey?" asked the man. "He told me they found a "mass" of some kind in her jaw...he showed me the X-ray, and it looked like a shadow had extended over a couple of her teeth as well. He said he has no idea what he is dealing with, and he wants me to get into a specialist as quickly as possible. I could barely see it on the picture, but he insisted that we bring her there in the morning. Sounds like they may want to do a biopsy." The man was speechless. This was his little girl...Daddy's little girl. Tears rolled down his cheeks, as he gathered his thoughts. And the night soon went still…

The man's plane touched down, as he scrambled to retrieve his bags. He gathered his belongings and quickly made it to his car. The thought of his little girl going under the knife, without any agreed-upon game plan, just didn't seem right to him. Wasn't the diagnosis supposed to come before the surgery? How could he and his wife get the answers they so desperately needed at this point? They would soon be moving to a brand new city, and that was tough enough. And now they had to deal with this…who could they turn to for guidance and who could possibly understand what they were going through? He pulled into his driveway and quickly made it through the garage door. His wife was waiting for him…they hugged one another, as they found themselves going down a path of no return. Fear embraced both of them, as they soon became one. Tears began to flow, as the man gently whispered, "It's going to be ok, honey. We will find a way to do the right thing. We will get our little girl to the right physician….someone who has been there before. We need to find the right person quickly…and we will." The two of them quickly regained their composure, despite the fact that sleep had not been part of their vocabulary since the initial dental visit nearly 48 hours earlier. This was not the time or place to show their emotions, as their two daughters watched the activity from the other room. Immediately, they gathered their thoughts and assessed their next move. Then it hit him...his uncle would know where to turn. He was one of the most prominent dentists in the Pacific Northwest. The man got on the phone and tracked him down. He explained the sequence of events and then waited for a response. After careful deliberation, his uncle had a plan. It would be extremely important for them to get the X-rays in front of the right team. Within 48 hours, a team of specialists was assembled and reviewing the X-rays. The waiting game was about to begin...and the prognosis did not look good.

"I believe it is an ameloblastic fibroma, and it needs to be removed quickly," stated the radiologist. He had seen these before and knew they were risky...and very unpredictable as well. The problem was twofold. First of all, because they were rare, there just wasn't a lot of experience treating them if they, in fact, came back malignant. The tumor was positioned in a way that imposed considerable threat to the little girl, and he knew it. The second problem was the most critical one at this juncture. Who in the world was qualified to take this cystic "mass" out? There were only a handful of individuals in the country who had ever seen these before... and only a couple who had actually performed the procedure that needed to take place. The radiologist thought for a moment about the options that were in front of him. He consulted with his team and decided his recommendation would be an old colleague who lived in Southern California. The man was an incredible surgeon who made his home at Children's Hospital, totally devoted to the kids who entered the hospital with shattered dreams and lifeless bodies. He was the kind of guy you would have operate on your own little girl, if confronted with the situation. He specialized in tumors because he felt this was his calling...his opportunity to truly make a difference. He tackled the really tough cases, and he knew this would be one of them. The family now realized "why" they were moving from the comfort of their Rocky Mountain home to the uncertainty of Southern California. The fact of the matter was that they had no idea this tumor would drive them closer to the answers they had been searching for...their little girl would soon meet the man who would determine her fate.

The oral surgeon reviewed the X-rays, as he prepared for the first of many consultations. As he walked into the exam room, the family immediately turned to him for answers. The little girl smiled and introduced herself. He could sense right away that there was something very special about this little girl. She carried herself with humility and grace, and she exuded a confidence that can only be experienced through divine faith. Her maturity and can-do positive attitude was evident from the time he reached out and felt her warm little hand. One thing was for certain…he would never forget this little girl. Her little sister sat in the chair next to her and listened to him describe her prognosis. He was careful with his words, as he juggled the delicate balance between reality and potential fear of the unknown. Although he was one of the few surgeons who had experience with these types of tumors, he realized in his heart of hearts that there was still a high level of uncertainty. For the first time in her life, the little girl was genuinely scared for her big sister's life. After all, this was not only her sister they were talking about. It was her best friend as well…

He pulled up his chair and walked through the surgery that awaited them. This was the tough part of his job. He could remember back in medical school when he was told numerous times to stay focused on the procedure and not the patient. Theoretically, he could understand the logic behind this directive. However, this was not the reality of the situation for him. These kids were his family, and the "frank" discussions that needed to take place just never seemed to get any easier. How can you not get emotionally attached to the kids, he thought, as he mapped out every detail. One of the things he firmly believed in was the involvement of the entire family when it came to decisions like the one they were about to face. The little girl listened intently to the scenario he described. She felt like she was a part of the overall plan that was about to be put into action…and she liked that a lot. Over the coming weeks, the family worked closely with the surgeon, as they tackled one challenge at a time. After a CAT Scan and an MRI, the surgeon was confident he had finally located the entire mass. This one was different than others he had seen…the viscosity level of the fluid that appeared to be on the inside of the growth made it unclear as to whether it was a cyst or a tumor. This was a critical piece of the equation, as it would dictate the number of surgeries that needed to take place. In addition, it was difficult to tell how large the growth was…it was positioned on the side of the jaw and had wrapped itself around the three lower teeth as well. The surgeon's main concern right now involved the removal of the entire growth. Once removed, they would need to biopsy it and see if it was benign or malignant. Fortunately, the waiting game would soon be coming to an end. The family had been living through this emotional roller coaster for over two months now, and they were ready to move on. Within 48 hours, she would be in surgery at Children's Hospital, and the family would finally have the answers they needed.

The surgeon did everything in his power to comfort their thoughts. As he walked out of the exam room, he took a deep breath. He knew this wasn't going to be easy.

On the day of the surgery, the family got to the hospital at around 3:00 p.m. Based on the surgeon's final assessment, he felt confident in his decision to go after the entire mass in one fell swoop. He needed to be aggressive, as he knew it could localize and grow once again if active cells were left behind. Surgery was slated for 5:15 p.m.; therefore, they had plenty of time to get settled in before the procedure would begin. The admittance process went smoothly; however, it was very unsettling for the family, as they mentally prepared for the events to come. Vital signs were taken, as the girl changed into her soft, little gown that would keep her body warm during the five-hour procedure. The waiting room became very still, as the family watched the clock slowly tick down. They were alone now, as they sat and waited for the anesthesiologist to arrive. He would soon explain to the family the risks associated with sedating the little girl, and the onset of action she would experience with the drug he administered. His ability to make the anesthetic sound relatively harmless and reassuring gave the little girl even more confidence than before he entered the room. He was a very nice man, she thought, as she listened to his every word. It was now about 5:00 p.m., and he was ready to take their little girl into the other section of the surgery department. The family would not be permitted to go into the next room so this was it…this would be the last time they would see her until it was over. They needed one last minute together before they said good-bye. They closed their eyes, held hands, and prayed for the Lord's strength. Tears welled up in Mom and Dad's eyes, as they could feel the warmth of their little girl's hands. Their youngest daughter remained still and prayed with all her might. They stood up and approached the door to where the anesthesiologist was waiting…they didn't want to say good-bye, but they knew they had to. The girl reached out her hands one last time as Mom, Dad, and little sister clutched her with everything they had. She said nothing but instead tapped her family three times…and they, in turn, returned the three taps with four. With that, they said, "I love you too," as they watched their little girl walk down the corridor toward the room. The doctor held out his hand, as Mom and Dad watched from afar. They couldn't cross that line, but oh, how they wanted to run after her and give her one last hug. As she reached the end of the hallway, the little girl turned around and gave them one last smile. She was gone…and they were all alone.

The little girl in this story was our daughter. I remember the sequence of events like it was yesterday. Without a doubt, this situation immediately rocked our world. Realizing just how uncertain our lives are each and every day should instill an incredible sense of urgency to do something for those we care about today. You see...these life-changing events can happen quickly, and before you know it, you are scrambling to make up for lost time. This is exactly what happened to me. I was thrown into an immediate tailspin, and the only one who could pull me out of it was God. My faith has grown deeper in Him because of what He did for our family...how can I ever repay Him? I hope and pray this book is a good start...

Pathway of Encouragement

We have since taken our daughter back to Children's Hospital each year for the past five years, and there has been no sign of any relapse regarding the tumor. Her jaw has been completely rebuilt with a product that was used to help start the healing process. Despite the fact that we had a miraculous series of events to get us to the point we are at right now, the wounds are definitely still fresh. There are times when my wife and I find ourselves reflecting back on what happened, and immediately we lose our sense of composure and begin to cry once again. I am sure everyone can relate to this feeling of helplessness, as all of us have had to deal with painful events in our lives. For us, God reached down and touched our family on that October day, and the feeling was unlike anything we had ever been through before. I remember waiting for our surgeon to tell us whether the tumor was benign or malignant…it seemed like an eternity. Finally, he surfaced with the word that we needed to hear, and our entire bodies went numb. The feeling of absolute vulnerability is one I never want to forget again. Because…with this remembrance of vulnerability comes a sense of urgency as well. As painful as it can be, I never want to forget just how dependent we were on the Lord that day when our little girl was in surgery. I have honestly tried to capture that feeling and not forget what it was like to turn to God for help…and ultimately to praise Him as well, regardless of the circumstance. I truly believe that if we can live our lives every day with this absolute reverence for Him, we will grow exponentially in our faith.

Without a doubt, the time is now for all of us to give our loved ones the "three taps" they so rightly deserve and so desperately need. We simply cannot wait for tomorrow… for tomorrow may be too late. Jesus exemplified the ultimate form of suffering for all of us when He died on the cross for our sins. The world will continue to inflict suffering on all of us in our lives...this is a given. However, no matter how bad things are, we need to focus on the fact that God is the only one who knows what our limitations entail. He will never allow us more than we can handle...and we need to believe this with all our heart! Doing so will give us the necessary peace we need when it seems like we cannot go on any longer. Please do not give up when the walls are closing in on you... focus on Him, and they will begin to open up once again. Suffering is something all of us will do, different levels of pain for each of us. When our heart is broken, and we feel like we cannot go on any longer, this is where we need to turn to Him for strength. None of us is strong enough to go through this pain and suffering alone. Before our daughter got sick, I turned to God a lot, but more out of necessity than praise. When I was about to tackle a challenge of whatever kind, I asked Him for help. Now, I try to turn to Him each and every day and thank Him for what He has done in my life, regardless of the situation I am in. When I look around and see all the pain and suffering in this world, I realize just how blessed I really am. I have honestly looked at every day of my life, since our daughter got sick, differently than I did before...because I now know what it is like to feel totally helpless. That helplessness made me realize that He is always there for me...and He will never let me down.

Chapter Two

"His Father's Eyes"

Humility...Matthew 23:12
"For whoever exalts himself will be humbled, and whoever humbles himself will be exalted."

The sun beat down on his darkened face, as the young boy knew it would be another busy day. You see... every day was hectic at his house. Not just your average chores for a boy of 12, but instead an immediate jump into adulthood that not many his age would ever reach in a lifetime. His responsibilities at home were enormous, as his parents had searched to him for advice in just about everything they encountered. The boy was gifted in almost everything he did, including carpentry and oratory skills unmatched by anyone else in his small village. As he reached for his trousers, he could feel the sun take hold of his body and the warmth begin to consume him. He smiled and began to move toward the door. His day was about to begin...

"Son...we need you to go into the city and fetch the additional grain needed in order to bake enough bread for the coming month," said his mother, as she greeted him at the door. "Yes, Mother...I will go as soon as I have checked on all the sheep out back. I want to make sure each of them made it through the night safe and sound." His mother smiled, as she watched him quickly make his way out the front door. Her son was growing up right in front of her eyes, and he would soon become a man. She wasn't quite ready for this, but oh, how proud she was of him. The future frightened her, and she wasn't sure why. Some day, the whole world would know...but would they accept him? Some would...but others would fall away and search for answers in the flesh.

The boy yelled good-bye, as he made his way down the winding road toward the city. His journey would soon be interrupted by an old woman, who was in desperate need of his help. The woman had recently lost her husband and had literally been left out in the cold, with not one friend to her name. Her husband had died instantly, and he had done nothing to prepare her for a life without him. The boy had been on his trip to the city for not more than 20 minutes when he came across her lying on the side of the road. Why was she there...was she in need of his help, or was she one of the city's peddlers trying to lure him into a trap? His intuition was sound and his heart was pure, so he walked over to her to see if she was ok. "Are you all right, ma'am? It looks like you have been injured. What can I do to help you?" The woman reached down, grabbed her leg, and proceeded to show the young boy what had happened. Her leg had somehow been injured, and she would be left to die if he decided to move on. "I will get you to someone who can repair your damaged leg," he said. And with that, he lifted the woman to her feet and took her up the hill to the small village she called home. From behind the padded shelter came the woman's brother. He was a bitter old man, and he began to scream at the young boy. "What are you doing here?" he shouted. "We were all hoping she would just go away and die, and now my sister will be taking up space here once again. Get out of here before I hurt you real bad." The boy simply nodded his head and looked into the woman's eyes, as she crawled into her brother's home. Her head turned away in shame, and she said nothing. Her life had been saved, but the boy was being punished for his actions. The door slammed in his face, as he turned away. His act of kindness would not be recognized, but he would move on...and he would not change.

He was now about halfway through his journey, and as he came to the bend in the road, the young boy heard a whimper that seemed to come from up around a rock that had nestled its way into the side of the hill. The boy took a deep breath and slowly peeked over the top of the weathered stone. A small fawn had somehow found its way into the rock and had slipped down to the bottom of the crevice that engulfed its lower leg. As the boy began to move closer, he heard something in the trees and slowly turned to see where the noise was coming from. Out from behind the trees stood the most beautiful deer the boy had ever seen. The fawn's mother was scared for her baby's safety, and the boy was viewed as a threat. Her eyes pierced through him, as she slowly sized up her target. He would die for what he had done to her little baby, she thought. But then, she was caught totally off guard by the actions of the boy. He dove between the rocks, and he began to pull with all his strength. Suddenly, the stone that had wedged her baby's leg chipped away...and her little one was set free. Up jumped the fawn, and within seconds, the two darted off into the distance, leaving the boy resting on his side near the rock that nearly consumed his unknown friend. As he wiped away the sweat from his brow, he reached down and picked up his hat.

The trees were silent, and he felt all alone. But...he knew he wasn't. His Father was always with him.

The boy made his way down the trail, as he stayed on course for the next two hours without any disruptions. He was slowly approaching the city and only had limited time before the market would close. He would need to start running in order to make it in time to secure his mother's grain. As he began to make it into the neighborhood just outside the market, he immediately became fixated on the argument that was taking place next to the cobblestone building near the side of the road. "You are just an old man without any skills. If you don't fix this door before sundown, I will not only take your job, but I will also take your firstborn daughter as well." "No, No, No!"...cried the old man, but the young foreman just shook his head and walked away. "You have very little time, old man. I will be back as soon as the sun goes down to collect my pay." The young boy slowed down, as he needed to make a quick decision. His mother needed the grain; however, he couldn't leave this man alone. You see...carpentry was one of the many gifts he had been given, and now he would use it as he knew best. He reached down and helped the man to his feet. The boy said nothing. He spoke with his actions and proceeded to reach for the mallet. Within 30 minutes, he had built a door that was absolutely perfect. With all his strength, he pounded in the last nail and turned to find the old man…but he was gone. No thanks from anyone…nothing. The boy slowly picked himself up and turned to look behind him. The foreman's shadow walked in the distance, and the boy could hear him reveling in disgust. The old man, and his daughter, had been spared once again. As the boy slowly reached down and picked up the last nail, his hands began to shake. Nobody was there to see him, but he could feel an enormous amount of fear engulf his body for what felt like an eternity. He fell to the ground and began to search for answers…and blood began to slowly drip to the ground below him.

The boy sat down and began to weep. Nobody saw him, but he could feel his Father looking down upon his tired body. His tears flowed, as he gently rubbed his hands. As the boy reflected on his journey that day, he knew this was just the beginning. For the next 21 years, the boy would never lose his compassion for people, and he would help everyone around him regardless of what it would cost. He took a deep breath and looked up into the sky and said, "Father, I am scared…but I know why I am here." His Father's eyes slowly opened and down came his answer. The young boy wiped the raindrops from his forehead, as he could feel the warmth of his Father's arms slowly reach around him. He felt safe and slowly closed his eyes. The boy's journey, for all of us, was about to begin. However, just like his trip to the village that day, many here would not take notice.

Pathway of Encouragement

Every day, we have all been given the power to persevere and the opportunity to be humble in all that we do. God's grace has covered us and will continue to cover us until our last days on earth. We cannot ever think that all the little things we do go unnoticed…because God sees everything. Just like the young boy heading to the village, He watches us and loves us for who we are. He is with us…we must continue to fight the fight because everything we do is for Him. Do not get discouraged because the world does not take notice. Gaining recognition in the eyes of man is not why we are here. Man will ultimately disappoint us; however, God never will.

Humility is a lost art in today's world. Most men and women are out to please others and impress those around them for all the wrong reasons. In most cases, this lack of humility is a true reflection of the insecurity that develops in all of us at an early age. So, how do we rise above all this and attain true humility in the eyes of the Lord? Simply put, we need to give all the glory to Him. The minute we start to take credit for what He has done for us, we are in big trouble! We see it all the time in our personal lives. Athletes and entertainers, who continually refer to themselves as the greatest of all time, surround us and take all the credit for what they have done. Co-workers who accept the accolades for successful projects quickly deflect any blame for disappointing results. Whatever happened to sharing the credit, and the blame, for events that consume our daily lives? Humility is a gift that needs to be nurtured at an early age. There is nothing more precious than a child who uncharacteristically passes all the credit on to others. However, it is important for us to reinforce this behavior as soon as it happens. In most cases, children grow into young adults who have their eyes focused on the wrong target. Worldly pressure pushes many down a path of materialism and false idols. This is where we as adults and parents really need to keep our kids grounded. However, we also need to lead by example. Humility is something we need to teach through our actions, not our words. Giving the glory to God, in all that we do, will allow us to remain focused on Him and steadfast in His ways…

Chapter Three

"The Last One Chosen"

Seeds of Strength...Revelation 21:7
"He who overcomes will inherit all this, and I will be his God and he will be my son."

Nick Watson had one last corner before he pulled into the parking garage. Throughout the evening, the weather had turned for the worse, and he felt very fortunate to have made it into the office before any of his employees. He had envisioned this day for a very long time, and he certainly didn't want to be late for what was about to begin. Nick knew the ride later that morning would be almost impossible to navigate, and he was happy to be inside where it was warm. He shut the car door and made it quickly to the elevator door. As Nick climbed toward the 23rd floor, he thought about all he had done...and all the blessings this

Christmas season would bring upon him and his family. The elevator door opened, and Nick proceeded down the corridor to his office. Two turns to the right and there he was...the corner suite of the MacArthur Office Complex. How in the world did he ever end up here? He made it to his desk and turned his chair around toward the window. The redness of the sun on this December morning seemed to burn through his soul and reach into his heart. He closed his eyes and felt its warmth start to radiate through the large window outside. Nick began to reflect on a time many years ago and slowly began to whisper to himself, "Please, don't hit me anymore... I am sorry. It won't ever happen again." He reached into his top drawer and pulled out a tissue. Slowly, he dabbed the corner of his eye and tried to keep the tear from racing down his face. Nick took a deep breath and quickly turned away from the window. On this morning, like so many others, the beauty of the sun somehow took a back seat to the pain that gripped him like a vice. Looking back at his life was a dangerous move, and he knew it. Satan's job was to curtail his inner strength by taking him back, and Nick couldn't let this happen. Running Watson Enterprises had nothing to do with the real reason Nick was here...his job today was much bigger than that. This was a day he had dreamed about for many years, as he tried to gather his composure and quickly move his mind toward the present. He opened the top drawer of his desk and took out the small envelope. "I will love you forever...always look forward, never look back. For God has given you this day for a reason...now go out and make a difference." Nick took a deep breath...he needed to somehow get himself together.

John quickly reached over to wipe her tears down, as Sarah was feeling the pain of being rejected once again. The adoption was nullified at the very last moment and, for yet another Christmas, the couple would be alone. For eight years now, they had been hoping and praying for the gift that would make their lives complete. However, the obstacles placed in front of adopting children from overseas were enormous. John and Sarah had tried nearly everything In their power to get past the regulations that had been placed in front of them, but nothing seemed to go their way. Unbearable frustration was consuming them, and they could feel their marriage starting to unravel. Sarah's inability to have children of her own was creating a wedge between her and the only man she had ever truly loved. Her obsession to find a child had started to consume her, and she felt deeply in her heart that God would someday find them that perfect match. How had this one gone wrong? The papers had been checked over repeatedly, and it looked like they finally had their wish. The boy had been cleared, but something had gotten in the way just as everything was being finalized. Why? Sarah just had to know...she had to give it one last try.

Slowly, the door closed behind him, as he took his first step toward the attic. The metal rod dragged along the side of the wall and methodically tapped against each of the many crevices that lined the staircase. The boots were loud and the sound of them getting closer to the door seemed to freeze time like a hollowed grave. The boy lay motionless in the dark corner hoping the noise would stop; however, he knew there would be more to come. This ritual had started nearly two years earlier, as the eight year old had become accustomed to what was in store for him. The steps grew louder, as he began to count them one-by-one. Sixteen, seventeen, eighteen, nineteen, twenty...the boots would soon reach the end of the two-story journey. "Nicolai...come out from your corner," whispered the dark raspy voice. "You are my little animal, and it is time for you to eat." Every night, the food would come...but so would the beatings. Some nights were worse than others. The man lashed out with the metal rod, as Nicolai lay motionless on the floor. The room was dark... and once again, little Nicolai Krushevsky would lie alone and wish he were dead. Why was he being treated this way? The orphanage was supposed to be a safe haven for kids without parents...but this was not the case at the Stonebrige Retreat for Boys. Nicolai had been there now since he was just two years old...the only place he had ever known. Oh, how he prayed for a real home, just like the one he dreamed of every night. Surely, places like that "couldn't be real" he thought. Oh, how he longed for just one night in a bed... sleeping without the metal rod.

Nicolai only had one friend at the home, Mr. August... "Augie" for short. Nicolai looked for him every day, and Augie would go out of his way to tend to Nicolai. Mr. August was in charge of all custodian work at Stonebridge. He could still remember the day that little Nicolai was dropped off at the front door by his parents. Nicolai now laid claim to being the longest serving resident at Stonebridge Retreat for Boys, and he had seen just about everything one could imagine. The man in the boots was known as the Rat, and every night Nicolai thought about how he would like to dispose of this monster. The Rat was a wicked man, and the beatings were his way of controlling the young boy. But Nicolai was different...as the rod routinely dug deep into his back; he closed his eyes and clenched his teeth. There were no tears, as the pain had turned into anger long ago. He would live for another day...a new day, he thought. And someday, his dreams would have happy endings, and the Rat would be gone. Every evening, Augie would wait until the Rat would leave, and then he would sneak back up the staircase toward Nicolai's room. Having access to all the doors in the building, Mr. August would finally make his way to where Nicolai would be lying down. His hands would gently rub the bruised shoulders, and slowly, the pain would begin to subside. Augie would tell Nicolai about happy things... whatever it took to get his mind off of what just happened. "Hang in there, Nicolai, I promise I will get you out of here soon." Nicolai smiled and closed his eyes. "I know you will, Augie. Please, help me...I am starting to feel very tired." He fell asleep and began to dream once again. Somehow, Augie had once again taken his mind off the Rat...for this night anyway. He had to find a way to get Nicolai out of this nightmare before it was too late. He could sense that little Nicolai was living on borrowed time. The beatings were finally taking their toll on him, and Augie knew it. Nicolai's tears had stopped flowing long ago, but Augie's were there every night. He turned his head away from Nicolai and put his head down. His heart, along with Nicolai's will, was starting to break. Somehow, both needed to be fixed soon, or they would be gone forever.

And...then it arrived. The letter was delivered and Sarah began to shake, as she tried to open the seal. John reached over and held her hand. The envelope was postmarked from Tatieska, Russia, and both of them knew this could be it. Sarah began to read the note and could feel her heart race:

Dear Ma'am,

    I have been praying for a long time about the heart of a young boy…a boy who has been given a tremendous gift. He is currently in need of loving parents because his parents decided years ago that he was not part of their plan. The boy lives here at Stonebridge Retreat for Boys, an orphanage just 50 miles north of Moscow. I have seen other boys taken out of Stonebridge, but it only happens when you come in person with cash-in-hand. I read through your last letter, and I am certain the boy here is the answer to your prayers. Do not attempt to call or write…just come here fast! The boy is getting weak, and his days here are numbered. Your arrival will certainly give him the life he so richly deserves. Papers will be signed and everything will be approved, but you need to move fast. I will be looking for you upon your arrival. Krushevsky is his name…

God Bless,
AJR

Sarah looked at John and both felt as if the Lord was leading them to the young boy. "Let's pack our bags, dear. I really believe this is the one. We need to get to that boy." All John could do was nod his head in agreement, as he could feel the same desire to find him fast. "Honey, we will go after him, but this is it. Both of us have lived for this day, but we cannot continue down this path if it doesn't work out. We will do everything in our power to find the boy, but then this is it. If it is meant to be, it will happen. If not, we need to move on and build our world together without him." Sarah knew John was right...she reached out and hugged him with everything she had. The man she had loved was there for her once again, and that was all she needed. "Now, let's go get that boy!" John said, as they ran out of the house.

The car wove in and out of the heavy traffic, as it sped away from the airport. "Please, take us to Stonebridge Retreat for Boys...it's an orphanage on the outskirts of town." "I know where it is, ma'am," said the driver. "I see couples like the two of you go out there all the time. Not all of them leave with what they want. Some leave happy, others leave sad. I do hope you are one of the happy ones." "Thank you so much," Sarah responded. Her heart was set on finding that boy...there was no way she was leaving without what she came for. The car came to a sudden stop and there it was...the structure of the buildings seemed to be outlined by the darkened sky around it. John and Sarah made their way to the front of the building, only to be greeted by the caretaker. "We are here to pick up our boy...his name is Krushevsky. We received our letter just two days ago saying he was here." "I know nothing of what you say," mumbled the man. "What, do you think you can just show up here and have boy? The boy is not here right now," he continued, in his well-scripted, garbled English. Just then, out stepped a man from behind the closed door. "Oh, you must be the couple from Chicago, here to get Nicolai?" John reached out to shake the old man's hand, and he immediately felt at peace. "Don't listen to old man," barked the caretaker. "He has no idea what he talk about...he just silly old man, and he knows nothing about what goes on here." "Oh, I know what goes on here," said Mr. August, "and that is why we are getting Nicolai out." The Rat had been exposed, and he knew it. "Go ahead and take him with you then...but I need my money first!" screamed the Rat. John and Sarah handed over the $10,000 and signed all the necessary papers. "Now, let us see our boy," said John, as he made his way toward the door.

Augie led John and Sarah up the corridor, and Sarah soon felt her heart begin to sink deep into her throat. She could feel the coldness of the room press upon her, as the damp air seemed to reach out and suffocate her every thought. Tears began to flow down her cheeks, as she made her way toward the darkened room. "Nicolai, we have visitors here to see you," whispered Augie. With that, Nicolai leaned around the corner and saw the two figures standing just outside his reach. "Who are these people, Augie?" "Nicolai, these are your new parents...they are here to take you home." John reached down and slowly put his arm on Nicolai's shoulder, only to have him pull away. "It's ok, son...we understand. Augie has told us all about you, and we are here to make sure you are never hurt again. He has blessed us with the opportunity to meet you and take you with us, away from this place for good." Nicolai stood up and began to smile. It had been a long time since he felt this way...and his face felt different. The pain began to go away, as he truly felt like this was his chance to get away and start over. "You really want to be my mom and dad?" questioned Nicolai. "We love you, Nicolai,"...and with that, Sarah turned around and reached out to where Augie was just seconds before...but he was gone. It was as if he had disappeared. This would be the last time Nicolai ever saw his old friend, but he knew it was only because of him that he finally found a home. A home he could truly call his own...

Nick looked out at the crowd and realized his dream had finally come true. Watson Enterprises had reached their lifelong goal...$100 M raised for OCA (Orphanages Club of America). It had been a long road, but his vision was now a reality. As Nick began to address the crowd, he could feel the presence of the Holy Spirit grip his every word...

"We are here today for one reason...and one reason only. This ceremony is all about the kids. Kids are brought into this world to be loved, and we must never forget this. If we do, then our whole society will slip into mediocrity, and we will have nothing to show for it. The more we love the kids, the more we all benefit. If we turn our backs on them, then they will, in fact, turn their backs on their kids too...and the vicious cycle is well on its way to destruction. I thank each and every one of you today. Through your contribution and commitment, we have finally reached a milestone. $100 M can help with our infrastructure and ultimately put the OCA foundation in place, but without individual love for the kids, it means nothing. We will all suffer a slow and painful death if we don't have a heart for the kids...kids who desperately need us. For nothing is more precious than the smile and passion of a young child. Together, we can make sure this flame never burns out...but instead magnifies itself, as life takes hold and starts to grow. For in this world, kids are abused every day…and with it, we all die a little bit at a time as well. We simply cannot let this happen or tolerate its ugly stain on who we are and what we stand for. Watson Enterprises is blessed to be affiliated with the OCA and for this reason; it is our distinct privilege to have the opportunity to be here with you today. Our fight has only just begun, and we will never stop until we reach out and touch every child we possibly can. Thank you for your time here today…and thank you for your love. I know the kids thank you too!"

Nick made his way down through the crowd and slowly found his way to the back of the auditorium. He felt embarrassed by the attention he was receiving, and he wanted to deflect the credit that seemed to be directed his way. As he started to work his way toward the door, he glanced over to his left side and saw the old man sitting in his wheelchair. His eyes immediately met the old man's, as everything seemed to be moving in slow motion. He stopped in his tracks and began to move slowly toward him. The old man reached out his arms and Nick could feel the strength of his grip around his shoulders. The man pulled Nick's face toward the side of his chin and began to whisper in his ear. "I am very proud of you, Nicolai. I knew you would make it." Nick could feel his eyes start to swell up with tears, as he looked directly into the old man's eyes…"God Bless you, Augie. I wouldn't be here today if it wasn't for you."

With tears in their eyes, the two men held each other tight once again. This was a special day for both of them…for Stonebridge Retreat was now officially dead…and it would never haunt either of them ever again.

Pathway of Encouragement

Our actions speak louder than words in all that we do. How we treat our kids is no exception. Whenever we can…we need to reach out and hug our kids. Nothing we can do is more powerful in the eyes of a child than that of a hug…for hugs represent love. You can never give back a hug, and you can never take one away. They don't cost any money, and they certainly don't take much time…but nothing we do is more important. We don't have to talk, and we don't have to think…so why don't we do it more often? Millions of kids are being abused right now; despicable things are being done to the children of God. What can we do? We can get involved. Why do we continually turn our heads when the pain is on the other side of the room? We have seen children just like Nicolai rise above the world's continual oppression and do incredible things with their lives. We must recognize that our future is in the hands of our most precious resource... the kids. If we fail to get involved and recognize this, all of us will pay the price. Just like Augie did in "The Last One Chosen", don't ever give up on these kids! He believed in Nicolai, and the impact was felt by all. He did not turn his back, and soon the Rat was exposed. We need to look out for those who can't...God's children need to be protected and loved. Generations to come are depending on us to stop the abuse now...before it goes any further!

In addition, many adults today were a target of abuse as a child, and the pain they are going through continues to haunt them each and every day. This is where we as believers need to step up and help them get through their pain. Nothing we do or say will ever take away the pain, but we can be there as a friend...someone who will simply listen to their words and comfort their hearts. Abuse is highly prevalent in today's society, whether it be physical or mental. It is important for us to stop it now because the cycle truly is vicious, and in many cases, contagious from one generation to the next. Seeds of strength are extremely important for society to grow, as we need to make sure our children are nurtured and loved early on in life. In order for these seeds to grow, we as Christians need to provide the water. They are our future... we need to treat them as such.

Chapter Four

"Back of Mind"

Forgiveness...1 John 1:9-10
"If we confess our sins, he is faithful and just and will forgive us our sins and purify us from all unrighteousness. If we claim we have not sinned, we make him out to be a liar and his word has no place in our lives."

Charles Frye took a deep breath, as he prepared for his company's annual meeting. He was getting ready to deliver some terrific news to the shareholders of Frye Technologies Inc., as his company had just come off their 10th straight record-breaking year in a row. Their success in the telecom industry was unprecedented, especially since most of the industry had struggled terribly over the past decade. Charles and his Executive Team had experienced a tremendous amount of personal wealth over the past decade, and everyone in the industry looked at Frye Technologies as the envy of the industry. Charles had built his organization from scratch, as he epitomized the hard-working image his company had developed over the years. Charles felt as though he had done everything there was for him to do, yet there was still something missing. His continual search for peace was constantly hitting a dead-end, and today would be no different. As he closed his eyes and slowly began to meditate before his speech, he couldn't help but see her face. How was he to know? How was Charles to have known she would be there? He should have never done it, but he did. His secret could never get out...he moved toward the podium hoping this would all go away, and he would once again put his "game" face on. But what if it didn't go away...then what would he do? His mind raced, as he began to address his people...but what if his words meant nothing? Oh, how he would take peace over profits any day of the week...if only he could find a way. His mind began to take him back to that place of 30 years ago. A world that just wouldn't leave him alone...his personal demons were getting ready to play with his mind once again. After all, taking him back to that day was their favorite thing to do.

"Come on, Charlie, don't be a chicken. He is an old man who won't even notice we were there. I have been watching him for the past month, and he does the same thing every single night. He goes down to the grocery store at 7:00 p.m., and then he proceeds to spend the next 60 minutes there doing who knows what. His life is meaningless, and I am sure there isn't anyone around who even notices when he leaves or when he comes back. He usually gets back home at around 8:15 p.m., and then he meanders upstairs to the room in the back of his house. He spends the next 30 minutes or so walking back and forth from one side of the room to the other. I can see him through the window. I think the old man is nuts. It looks as if he is holding something in his arms, but who knows what in the world he is doing? Knowing him, he could be talking to his groceries! Bottom line is he has a routine that fits perfectly into our plans. We get in, we get out… and nobody knows we're there. Charlie…you gotta grow up and live a little. This will change our lives forever…let's do it. He is just an old man. Nobody will even notice. Trust me. I have been scouting out this place for us to make our move. We are a team, aren't we? The old man has money, Charlie. We take a couple hundred bucks, and that's it. He won't even notice it's missing. Do you want to be part of this or not?"

"I don't know, Raymond," said Charlie. "I just don't want to get in trouble. Sure…I would love to have a couple hundred bucks, but what if something goes wrong. I mean, what if we get caught? We could go to juvenile jail or something. I heard that place downtown is really bad. I know a few kids from school who were put down there, and they were super mean kids. I definitely don't want to end up down there with them, that's for sure."

"Charlie…let me spell this out for you. I am moving on this tomorrow night. You go home tonight and think long and hard about this. I have seen where you live, Charlie, and I hate to break it to you buddy, but your parents aint actually rollin' in the dough. Your dad works his butt off and can't even buy a new car. And your mom…everyone knows your mom is a drunk, Charlie. You don't want to end up like them now, do you? You will never see a couple hundred dollars from them…or from that piddly little job you got down sweeping old man Jacobs' floor at his store. Let me know in the morning. I got a back-up plan that I will move on if you don't want the job. Your back-up is a good friend of mine, not as good as you, but I will bring him on board if you pull out. Your choice…let me know in the mornin' man. Later." With that, Raymond turned around and before Charlie could say anything, he was gone.

Charlie Frye was a good kid; he had always done what was right and what his parents wanted him to do. Charlie's father was a butcher down at the local Meat Block, working from dawn till dusk since Charlie was little. He never had a lot of time for Charlie, but Charlie knew why. Charlie's mother had struggled with alcohol for years, which had taken a toll not only on his father's peace of mind, but on their family finances as well. Charlie typically found himself staying away from home until after his dad arrived because he just couldn't bare to see his mom like that. On this particular evening, Charlie made his way up the driveway and went through the side door that led to his bedroom. His father had gotten home a short while before, so Charlie knew he could go to his room without being bothered by his mom. He set his books down and made his way over to the bed. He needed to really think about what Raymond had just said. He had nobody to talk to...and nobody to call. Raymond was a very bad influence, but he was right about one thing. Charlie would never see a couple hundred bucks from his parents, and he really could use the money. Maybe this one time would go unnoticed, and Charlie would be rich...and then he would never have to worry about sweeping old man Jacobs' floor ever again? A couple hundred bucks is a lot of money...especially to a 16-year old.

Raymond and Charlie hid behind the hedge that wrapped around the old man's yard. They watched to see if the old man would be heading to the store tonight or not. There was a part of Charlie that really didn't want him to come out that front door, as he could feel the sweat slowly forming on the top of his lip. Charlie looked over at Raymond and could sense that he was truly in his element. He was a bad kid... and he was really loving this. It was obvious that he had brought Charlie along for the ride. If something went wrong, there was no way he was taking the fall alone. Just then, the door began to open and out came the old man. He shuffled down the sidewalk and began to move toward the direction of the local grocery store, just like he had been doing for quite some time now. Raymond leaned over to Charlie and said, "Let's give him a couple minutes to get away, and then we will make our move. We can slip through the back door, and we'll be done with this in a couple of minutes. This is going to be fun." It wasn't any fun to Charlie...his heart was racing a hundred miles an hour. He was scared to death and really didn't want to do this. Why didn't he just tell Raymond no? His father had raised him better than this and always reinforced the importance of hard work. As much as Charlie wanted to say no, he found himself moving toward the back of the house along with Raymond. This was really happening...everything was moving way too fast.

Charles Frye looked out over the hundreds of shareholders that stood at his arrival. Everyone was so proud and appreciative of Charles. He had lined their empty pockets with the kind of money they had never seen before...he was a true hero in their eyes, as they screamed and shouted his name. This was unheard of at a shareholder's meeting, but this would turn out to be no ordinary meeting. Greed had set in, and Charles was simply the one that not only wet their appetite...he was the answer that quenched their thirst! As Charles began to settle down the crowd, he glanced over at the teleprompter, and it was as if everything immediately stood still. Her face overlay the words on the screen, and Charles could still feel her blue eyes seem to penetrate his soul. He had hoped the memory would go away, but it just kept getting more and more intense. He closed his eyes hoping she would disappear, but her image only got clearer on the screen. The crowd could sense that something was different with Charles today...it should have been the happiest day of his life. However, this was a man who was trying to deal with something far more difficult than corporate growth. His soul was being exposed, and he felt dirty inside.

Raymond slowly opened the screen door and reached for the knob that would lead them inside. Mr. Clark never locked the door...he had no reason to. He had been there for 47 years, and nothing ever happened to him. He felt perfectly safe, but this was all about to change. Raymond and

Charlie made their way into the kitchen. The kitchen was neatly organized and looked almost as if it had never been used. They entered into the small front room, and Charlie paused near the television set that was in the corner. Above the television was a picture of Mr. Clark on his wedding day. He was a good-looking, confident man, ready to the tackle the world. Charlie looked down at the date and did the math in his head...52 years was a long time to be married, he thought. Then, Charlie noticed something different about the picture. Mr. Clark's wife, who was seated next to him in the picture, was in a wheelchair. What a beautiful young woman, Charlie thought. For a moment, Charlie felt sad, as he couldn't help but wonder what might have happened to this beautiful young girl. He turned to point this out to Raymond, but he had already made his way to the staircase. He could care less about some silly, old picture...

Charlie followed Raymond upstairs. They quickly made their way into Mr. Clark's bedroom, where Raymond had been watching him through the window for the past couple of weeks. He grabbed Charlie by the collar and said, "This is the old man's room. He spends a lot of time up here. I am going to check out his dresser and everything else in here. You go and check out the other two rooms upstairs. We need to move on this quickly. If the old man comes back before we get out, we will need to take care of him." At that moment, Charlie realized just how dangerous Raymond Avila really was. He had no doubt in his mind that Raymond would, in fact, get rid of Mr. Clark if he came back and found them there. He did have to move quickly...the last thing he wanted to do was hurt the old man. Charlie went into the first room, and it was almost as if nobody had ever spent any time in there. Charlie went over to the dresser and opened the top drawer. Nothing. He opened the rest of the drawers, and nothing was there as well. It was as if nobody, other than Charlie, had ever set foot in the room. Charlie made his way down to the last room at the end of the hallway. He reached for the door knob...this would be the room that would change his life forever.

Raymond made his way through the drawers and became more and more irritated, as he continued to come up empty. Charlie could hear Raymond cursing and yelling in the other room. Raymond began to scream at the top of his lungs, as he kicked over the dresser and the night stand. "There is nothing in here. The old man was broke...nothing!" screamed Raymond. Then, he reached down and threw the mattress off the bed. He began to dig under the covers to see if the old man had left anything there at all. Raymond moved his arm up and down the length of the mattress, and then he came across a small box. He took the box out and sat down on the edge of the bed. He could feel a smile come over his face...

Charlie began to make his way into the second room. He stopped in his tracks. Wrapped in a thick, blue blanket and resting in the fetal position was a woman who lay motionless. Charlie slowly made his way over to the bed and, by the slight movement of her shoulders, he could tell she was still breathing. He couldn't see her face, but it was clear to him that she was very small in stature. One of her crippled hands rested on the pillow next to her head. Charlie wanted to reach down and make sure she was ok, but he was afraid to wake her. If Raymond found out the old woman was in there, Charlie knew he would finish her off. The last thing Raymond needed was an eye witness. Charlie realized he had to get back to Raymond before he found out the two of them were not alone. Quickly, Charlie made his way to the door. "Hey, Charlie, get back in here and see what I found. You aren't going to believe this!" With that, the woman began to roll over and slowly opened her eyes. Charlie turned back and their eyes met, hers ripping through his soul like a sharp knife. The woman didn't say anything...and neither did Charlie. Charlie put his index finger up to his mouth and whispered, "Shhh." The old woman slowly nodded her head in agreement, and she closed her eyes once again. With that, Charlie made his way back down the hallway toward Raymond.

"Look at this box, Charlie. The old man probably kept everything he owned in here...let's see what he left us." Raymond dumped the box out on the bed. He reached for the sealed envelope and ripped it open. His grin quickly disappeared, as he counted out the money. "$500.00...are you kidding me!" screamed Raymond. "The old man left us only $500.00 and a bunch of junk. Look at this stuff, just a bunch of junk!" Raymond handed $200.00 over to Charlie and screamed in frustration. "Let's get out of here, Raymond," said Charlie. "The old man is going to get back soon. We got what we wanted...he doesn't have anymore. Let's go." Raymond kicked the television and shattered the screen, as he was quickly getting out of control. Charlie glanced down at the bed and saw the little gold heart laying next to the old man's box. He read the inscription on the back..."In memory of Julie Clark - our beautiful gift from God". Charlie put the heart into his pocket and began to follow Raymond out the bedroom door. They quickly made their way to the top of the staircase, when Raymond turned to Charlie and said, "Did you check out the other two rooms up here?" Charlie could feel a lump in his throat, as he tried to maintain his composure. "There's nothing up here, Raymond. The old man didn't own anything except what you found. Now, let's get out of here before he gets back." Raymond stopped in his tracks and looked back at the rooms down the hallway. It may be a good idea to check it out for himself...

Charlie couldn't let this happen. He quickly went over to the window and turned back to Raymond saying, "I think the old man is at the end of the street and heading this way. He is going to be here soon, Raymond. We have got to get out of here." Raymond had already started down the hallway. He was just about ready to enter the room where Mrs. Clark was lying, when he heard Charlie call out to him, "Here he comes!" shouted Charlie. Raymond couldn't afford to get caught, so he quickly turned back toward the staircase and started down to the main floor of the house. The two of them ran through the kitchen and out the back door, neither of them turning back to see if the old man was close or not. Charlie knew they had time. He hadn't seen anything, but he knew just how dangerous Raymond was at that point. He ran as hard and as fast as he could, but no matter how fast he ran, he just couldn't get her face out of his mind.

George Clark made his way to the sidewalk and turned toward his house, just as he had done every night for the past 20 years. After all, he had to get his Millie her favorite dish.

She just loved roasted chicken, dumplings, and hot rolls. George would do anything for his Millie…she was all he had. It had been that way for a long time now. After Julie's accident, the Clark's household was never the same. George made his way to the front door and proceeded to walk inside. He stood in disbelief, as he immediately fell prey to the mess that awaited him. George threw the groceries on the floor and made his way to the staircase. "Millie, are you okay? I am here, Millie. George is right here!" George grabbed on to the banister and started up the staircase toward the bedrooms. He looked at his bedroom and began to breathe heavily, as he made his way toward Millie's room. His room was a shambles; his most treasured belongings thrown all over the room as if they were meaningless. Nothing could happen to his Millie…he had to get to her quickly. As George opened the door, he could see the outline of Millie's body with the blankets pulled over her head. He closed his eyes and said a prayer, as he reached to pull the blankets back. Millie's eyes were closed…George reached down to see if she was breathing, as he wiped his tears away. There was no movement…her body lay still.

Charles Frye looked out at the audience with trepidation because he knew that nobody in that room would ever forget this day…

"I come to you today as your President and CEO of Frye Technologies with a heavy heart. Each of you has given so much to this company, and you can all be very proud of your accomplishments this past year. Needless to say, in an environment where our competition continues to fall by the waist side, we continue to grow at record pace. Success like this can only happen through hard work and perseverance, a willingness to do whatever it takes to win. For that, I am grateful. Today, I must do something that has been weighing on my heart for many years now. I have always been very clear about my expectations. Our ability to focus on the future has been one of our greatest assets. The mindset here has always been that no matter what, we will never look back, and we will never rest on our laurels. However, in order for me to move forward today, I must momentarily look back and address an incident that has been in the back of my mind for years. If I were to die today, I feel as though my life would be empty because there is a hole in my heart that needs to be filled. What I am about to tell you today is my first step in a long process. Although I have been thinking about this moment for years, I come to you with an unscripted attempt at forgiveness...one that may fall on deaf ears and one that will undoubtedly raise more questions than answers today. I want to preface my words with a request of you, if I may be so bold. I am so sorry for what I did, and I do not expect you to forgive me today. However, in due time, I hope and pray that you will. I have asked God for His forgiveness, and I do believe in my heart that He has provided me with the strength I need to come forth. In order for me to secure the necessary peace to move on, God has also made it clear that I must face my actions of 30 years ago with honesty and grace. I must address my demons head-on, and that is what I am about to do now."

"Millie, sweetheart. It's George. I am here for you now, honey. Please, wake up. I am here to protect you." George reached down and put his arms around the only woman he had ever loved. He began to comb his fingers through her soft, grey hair, but his actions were only met by the stillness of the room. At that moment, George could feel his lifeblood begin to slowly evaporate. His love, his life...his "everything" had left his world. He fell to his knees and began to sob uncontrollably. His life, as he knew it, was over. They had grown up in the same neighborhood, and George had a crush on Millie from the first day he laid eyes on her. They went through grade school and high school together...and got married shortly thereafter. They had been inseparable for years; how would he go on without her? George could feel his heart slowly begin to break...

Later, it would be revealed that Millie was literally frightened to death on that tragic evening...a crime that would go unsolved. Millie's death would precede George's by only three months, as George would soon follow his best friend. The cause of his death was diagnosed as a broken heart. Their intruders would simply walk away, never get caught, and go on to lead different lives. Raymond Avila drifted from one city to another, finally dying in the arms of a fellow transient on the outskirts of Boston. Raymond would never atone for his actions of that evening; he simply went on to commit other similar crimes until his life abruptly ended at the early age of 25. Charlie Frye, on the other hand, went on to lead what seemed to be a textbook life...one that only dreams are made of. He married his college sweetheart, raised three beautiful children, and he had taken a company from scratch and had built a dynasty. The perfect life...at least, that is what everyone thought.

"30 years ago, almost to this day, I did something that I deeply regret. When I was 16 years old, I broke into a house where an elderly man and his wife lived. They never did anything bad to anybody. In fact, I never knew their actual names until after the incident. I had an accomplice, who at that time, had a great influence over me. I made a huge mistake by giving into the pressure he exerted on me. Having said that, I take full responsibility for my own actions. One night, we decided to break into the house of George and Millie Clark, as we knew Mr. Clark went to the grocery store every night at about the same time. Our goal was to get a couple of hundred easy dollars that night because neither of us had ever made money like that on our own. What we didn't know, at the time, was that Mr. Clark also had a wife who was in the house when we entered as well. We proceeded to go upstairs and I ended up finding Mrs. Clark in her bedroom, as my partner ransacked the rest of the house. It turned out that she had been confined to a wheelchair since her teenage years, when she was diagnosed with a rare form of rheumatoid arthritis. Mr. Clark took care of his wife for the better part of their 52 years together, and he loved her with all his heart. After we burglarized their home, it turned out that Mrs. Clark passed away shortly after we left. Although Mr. Clark claimed that his wife's death was solely related to the break-in, it was never proven that there was, in fact, a connection. The police treated it as if it was just a normal burglary; just one of many in the city that evening. The young man who broke into the house with me has since passed away. Mr. and Mrs. Clark are also gone; sometimes I wish I was gone as well. However, tonight I stand before you with a conviction in my heart to come clean on this once and for all. I fully expect the authorities to prosecute me to the fullest, but I am ready to face my sentence. For I know, that no matter what happens to me from this point forward, I will never have to carry this burden with me anymore. I wish I could do it all over again, as I would have stood before you many years ago. But…I didn't. Today, I ask you for your forgiveness, and I wish you all the very best. I love all of you, but I must face my sentence. For once, I cannot be selfish. I must do what is right by God." With that, Charles Frye reached into his pocket and pulled out the little heart and pressed it toward his lips. He kissed the heart…and he prayed. He slowly began to open his eyes, looked at the inscription, and whispered, "I am so sorry, Julie. Someday, I hope to meet you and your parents as well."

Charles Frye spent the next 15 years in the Massachusetts Correction Facility. He would go on to write that, "It was here where I finally found the peace I so desperately needed. The bars that surrounded me for those 15 years were not near as restrictive as the oppression that consumed my mind for the 30 years before. In the back of my mind, I could think of nothing but Millie Clark's beautiful, blue eyes…the eyes that I hope I will see again one day."

Upon his release, Charles Frye became a pastor and went on to lead a small church in rural Massachusetts. He died at the age of 91, and those around him said he preached with a passion and conviction that came straight from the Lord himself. He spoke on a variety of topics, but all would agree that his most powerful message was on the one he felt closest to…the topic of forgiveness. After all, it was undoubtedly the one he knew best.

Pathway of Encouragement

The quickest way to move forward in our lives is by asking for forgiveness. Burdens are lifted, no matter how heavy they are, and they should never be revisited because this is not God's way. Once we ask the Lord for forgiveness, it is important that we move on with our lives. Satan is all about going back in time and dragging us through the days when we were not walking with the Lord. However, once we have asked God for forgiveness, God insists that we move forward. We cannot further the kingdom of God by looking through the rear-view mirror. Ask for forgiveness and move on…because we all have work to do!

If we don't ask forgiveness, we can fall prey to the same paralyzing mindset that tortured Charles Frey. It is extremely important for us to trust that once we have asked God for His forgiveness, and we truly repent for our sins, that He wants us to move on. If we disobey Him and we continually revisit something that He has already forgiven us for, then we are committing a sin. God wants us to further His kingdom; however, we cannot do so if we are unable to accept the fact that He has forgiven us. Living in the past is highly unproductive...keep your head up and stay focused on the prize. This is what He wants us to do...pure and simple.

Chapter Five

"Eyes of Blue"

Grace…Psalm 145:8

"The Lord is gracious and compassionate, slow to anger and rich in love. The Lord is good to all; he has compassion on all he has made."

"How old are you, Gram?" asked the little boy. "I am 97 years old, Benjamin." "No way, Gram! Not even the trees are that old. How could you be so old and look so good, Gram?" asked Benjamin. "Why, thank you, Benjamin. I am starting to look my age, you know," smiled Grace. Oh, how she treasured her days with Benjamin. He was such a good boy, so innocent in a world that would soon be waiting to pounce on his naivety. She could only pray that he would be ready.

Grace had a feeling that this was not going to be a quick conversation with her one and only grandson, but oh, how she treasured these moments. Benjamin had a way of touching her soul, of making her feel young again. His inquisitive mind was always searching for the answers that sometimes were so hard to give. Today's discussion with her grandson would be different than before...she was about to go back to a place she had stayed away from for many years...a place that she needed to overcome. For if she truly wanted to find the absolute peace she so desperately longed for, this would be one of her final hurdles. Grace and Benjamin soon made their way to the living room and sat down on the sofa. Benjamin was about to take her down a path that had been dormant for years, a dead-end filled with pain that only surfaced when she met it head-on. Grace stayed away from this part of her past, but it was always there laughing in her face...daring her to take that step forward.

Benjamin: Do you mind if I ask you a few questions, Gram? I want to make sure that you don't leave me soon, and there is a lot I need to know about life. Who else could I possibly talk to with more experience than you? You know everything, Gram, and I know very little. Just think, if I hang out with you this whole summer, some of you just might rub off on me. That would be great, Gram. I sure hope it happens.

Gram: Well, you do have a point, Benjamin. I do have a lot of experience. What's on your mind today?

Benjamin: I worry about certain things, Gram, and they never seem to come true...but I still worry about them anyway. How do I turn off the "worry machine" rolling around in my head?

Gram: Well, I can see that you have some real tough questions in your head today, Benjamin. Learning not to worry is a very tough thing to do, but I learned a long time ago, that I need to trust God with all my worries and just let Him handle it.

Benjamin: And how do you know He can handle it?

Gram: Well, I have come to realize that He is able to see the whole picture, and He already knows what will happen before it actually does.

Benjamin: What do you mean, Gram? Are you saying that He knows the ending before it actually gets started?

Gram: Well, Benjamin, it is kind of like when you read a book. Have you ever gone to the end of the book and read it before you start the beginning?

Benjamin: I do that all the time, Gram. I like to know how it ends; that way, I know if I really want to read it or not.

Gram: Have you ever read the ending of the book, and then once you do, all the scary parts of the book don't seem to be all that scary anymore because you already know the ending is good?

Benjamin: Yeah, that happens every time, Gram! I read the ending, and then once I know what happens, I can enjoy the other pages as well.

Gram: Well, think of that book as representing all of your worries, Benjamin. Now, trust that God will take care of the ending, and that way, you can enjoy all of the pages.

Benjamin: And the pages are like every day that I live, right Gram?

Gram: That is right, Benjamin!

Benjamin: I sure hope I am a big book, and I end up having lots of pages just like you, Gram!

Gram: I hope you are a big book too.

Benjamin: So, Gram, if God has control over all the pages in my book, then I have nothing to worry about, right Gram? All the pages will be happy ones, right Gram?

Gram: Well, now you are getting into the real tough part of the book, Benjamin. You see, everyone is going to have sad pages in their book. And how you handle those sad pages will determine how long your book turns out to be.

Benjamin: Slow down, Gram...you're kind of losing me now. Remember, I am only 10 years old, Gram. Did you forget?

Gram: I'm sorry, Benjamin. What I mean is that how we handle the tough pages of our own book is really the key to living a long life.

Benjamin: Did you have any bad, scary pages in your book, Gram?

Gram: I sure did. However, I do everything I possibly can not to go back to those chapters in my life. I never turn the pages back because then I have to work twice as hard to get back to where I was before.

Benjamin: I understand exactly what you mean, Gram. My really good friend, Billy Talbert, had a puppy, and one day a terrible thing happened. Billy's mother backed up their car in the driveway, and Billy's puppy was sleeping under the back of the car because it was really hot out and there was shade next to the tire. Billy's mother accidently ran her over, and she died at the dog hospital that night. Her name was Bella. Billy was really sad and hasn't smiled ever since. I am sad, too, but I try as hard as I can not to think about it. Even though Bella wasn't my dog, I loved her too. So, that was a very sad page for both of us.

Gram: I am not going to tell you that getting through those sad pages is easy; those pages are always going to be there. You just need to find a way to get through them quickly because there will be good pages around the corner. However, if you don't move on, you will never notice the good ones.

Benjamin: I have had a lot of really good pages, Gram. I am only 10, and I bet I have had more good pages than almost everybody, except maybe you. I think I will just concentrate on my good pages from now on.

Gram: Now, you're getting the hang of it, Benjamin!

Benjamin: Today is one of my best pages ever, Gram.

Gram: Me too, Benjamin. Me too...

Benjamin: I hate to ask you this question, Gram, so if you don't want to answer it, I totally understand.

Gram: I will answer your question. Go ahead, sweetheart...

Benjamin: What was the happiest day in your book, Gram, and what was the saddest?

Taking a deep breath, Grace could feel her knees begin to shake. She closed her eyes and said a quick prayer. Going back in her own book wouldn't be easy, but it was something she needed to do. She was two years older than Benjamin is now when it happened, but it felt like it was just yesterday. This would be the last time she ever went back. One more time, she thought...for Benjamin. And for her as well...

Gram: This may take a few minutes, Benjamin. You see, my best day and my worst day were, in fact, the same day, one that changed my life forever. At the time, it didn't seem like it was my best day because the emptiness I went through was indescribable. It made me realize that sometimes you need to go through horrific pain like this before you can truly proclaim your faith. Getting through these difficult times is impossible on your own...I came to realize this on the day I am about to share with you.

Benjamin: You don't have to go back in your book, Gram...I don't want to make you sad. That is the last thing I would ever do.

Gram: Thank you, Benjamin. I need to do this...I remember the day very well. Grace smiled, as she looked over at her grandson. He was such a good kid; truly a gift from God. Grace took a deep breath...the events of the day were still very fresh in her mind. It seemed like it was just yesterday...

I woke up that morning, and I still remember that it was one of the most beautiful days I had ever seen. I ran to the window and watched as the sun began to make its way over the hillside just beyond our backyard. Even though I had to go to school, I loved the fact that I was turning 12 on a

Friday. My mom and dad had promised me a special gift that weekend, and the anticipation was really starting to build. As I ran down the stairs, my dad was waiting for me at the kitchen table. As I jumped off the last stair and began to run as fast as I could toward him, I could tell that something just wasn't right with him. This was so unlike my dad...he always met me with a hug and a kiss at the bottom of the staircase, but today he seemed like he just wasn't the same man I knew. He looked over at me and told me I looked beautiful, but the spark in his eyes was gone. It was as if someone had sucked the life out of his body overnight. "Are you ok, Dad? You seem sad today...you do know it is my birthday, and that I am almost a teenager? One more year, and I will pretty much be a grown-up, you know. We have a big weekend planned...you didn't forget now, did you, Dad? Mama told me the three of us are going to do something real special, and she wouldn't tell me what it was. Do you think you could tell me, Dad...and I promise I won't say anything to her."

My dad slowly turned his head toward me, and I will never forget his expression. I felt like I was looking at a man who was dead, a body with no pulse. He tried to smile, but his mouth seemed to be frozen in time. His big, blue eyes began to tear up, and I had no idea why. Slowly, he whispered, "I love you," and he turned his head away. "Gracie!" my Mama yelled, and I turned and headed for the door. Before I had a chance to say anything to my dad, I was out the door and into the car. I remember driving away from the house wondering why my dad was so distraught, so motionless...and wondering why I left without telling him I loved him too. Within a matter of minutes, my birthday just didn't seem to be all that important to me. The sun was gaining strength, and I could feel the warmth begin to build on the back of my neck...but oh, how cold and scared I felt. I wanted my mom to turn back and check up on him, but I didn't do anything. Instead, I just sat there and said nothing. Before I knew it, my mom stopped the car, and we were in front of the school. "Gracie, you have yourself a great day. Happy Birthday, honey...remember, I am going to be over in Buckstown until late this afternoon, so you are going to need to take the bus home, ok? I have made arrangements for you, so just make sure you go straight home and get started on your homework. Your dad should be at home waiting for you when you get there. Once I get back, we can get everything ready for your birthday weekend, ok honey?" Suddenly, my birthday weekend meant nothing to me...my dad was on my heart, and it felt very heavy.

Benjamin reached over and touched his grandmother's hand. Gently, he wrapped his little fingers around hers and said, "You don't have to tell me anymore, Gram. I don't need to know...let's go for a walk, ok? I don't want to see you sad. You have the most beautiful, blue eyes in the world, Gram...I don't want to see them turn red." Grace reached down and put her arm around Benjamin and replied, "I appreciate that, Benjamin. However, if I don't talk about this now, I may never get another chance. This is the one thing that has always scared me, and I need to address it and move on." "Ok, Gram, I understand," said Benjamin. "I will listen to you...you just need to know that it is ok if you stop this story. I know how it is to be scared. You don't have to be scared, Gram."

I went through my day, and I remember nobody at school even knew it was my birthday. My day had slowly gone from one of joy to one of sadness. The bell rang, and I made my way out the front of the school and toward the bus. I went to the back of the bus and sat down. There was a lot of activity around me, but it was almost as if I was invisible. Nobody noticed me...I felt lost, and all I wanted to do was be with my dad. I wanted to hold him tight and tell him I love him too. The bus made its way down the road and took a right turn up toward our home. It stopped at the corner of our street, as I quickly went to the front of the bus. I turned to say good-bye to all the kids, but nobody was looking my way. I remember looking over at the bus driver, Mr. Wilkens, to see if he noticed me, but he was staring off into the distance as well. I got off the bus, and it quickly pulled away. I remember watching the bus leave our street and, before I knew it, I was standing there all alone. I ran as fast as I could to get to the house, so I could give my dad that hug I had been thinking about all day long. Oh, how I wanted to tell him that I loved him, and that everything was going to be ok. I ran around the back of the house and opened the door.

I made my way through the kitchen, when suddenly everything seemed to move in slow motion. I threw my books on the kitchen table and went out to the front room. Nobody was there, and I remember how the stillness of the room suddenly felt like it was suffocating me. I began to panic and yell for my dad, but there was no answer in return. I ran upstairs to see if he was there, but there was nobody. I went into my parent's bedroom, fearful of what I may find… but nothing was there as well. The only room I didn't check on was mine. I walked slowly down the hallway, and for whatever reason, I began to shake. Something was waiting for me on the other side of the door; my hands quivered as I reached for the door knob. I opened the door, and there it was…waiting for me on my bed.

I remember sitting down on my bed and slowly reaching for the note that was next to my pillow. *Gracie My Angel* was written on the front of the note...it was my father's handwriting. This message would change my life forever... it read:

Dear Gracie,

I am very sorry...I hope that someday you will forgive me for what I am about to do. I have decided to go away for awhile, as I need to have some time to myself. Everything in my life seems to be falling in on me, and I just need to clear my head and get my life together. I want you to know that it is nothing you have done, Gracie...it is me. My heart breaks when I think of you reading this letter, but I just cannot go on and be the father you deserve. You are such a beautiful person, Gracie, and I love you very much...but I cannot continue to go on this way. I hope to come back someday, and I do hope you will forgive me when I do. Please, remember that I will always love you. You will always be my little angel.

I love you,

Daddy

I fell to the floor and screamed out to the world..."No, No, No!" In a matter of minutes, my life was shattered. I could not believe that my dad was leaving me...that he would do this to me. Why? What had I done to deserve this...was it something I said? Was it because I didn't do my chores last weekend...what was it? I ran around the house yelling for him...I needed someone to hold me. I remember checking every room to see if he was there. But he wasn't...what was I going to do now? How could I go on? I needed my daddy, and he was gone. He had left me...

Benjamin reached over to his grandmother and slowly wiped the tear from her eye. "I am so sorry, Gram. I feel very bad that I asked you the question about your worst day. I had no idea it was going to be this horrible. We can stop now if you want to, Gram...you don't have to go on any longer with this story." Grace slowly began to smile, as she put her arms around Benjamin. "Thank you, sweetie. I am so grateful for you. You have such a big heart...don't ever lose it, ok? I am going to be all right. I need to keep going and finish my story. This will be the last time I ever speak of it again." "Ok, Gram," Benjamin said, "but if you want to stop, I will understand."

I frantically searched for my dad, but I found nothing. This couldn't be...I thought I was a good kid. I never did anything wrong. I remember sitting on the floor next to my bed sobbing uncontrollably, turning for someone to put their arms around me, but nobody was there. I was at the lowest point in my life...my dad had just left me, and for some unknown reason, I knew at that point in time he was never coming back. Then, without warning, I felt compelled to go to my window and look out at the hillside behind our house. Earlier that same day, I had looked out my bedroom window and met the sun as it welcomed my 12th birthday. In a matter of hours, my day had gone from one of hope to one of despair and pain. For a split second, as I looked out over the yard that led up to our back fence, I wanted to die. I didn't want to be there when my mom arrived, as I really believed that I was the reason for my dad's departure. My mind began to race, as I started to think about the easiest way for me to end the pain. I was terrified, as these thoughts had never made their way into my head before. I just wanted to be happy once again. I was on the verge of doing something really horrible, when I felt the presence of another person next to me in my room. This person would change my life forever...

    I closed my eyes and began to pray. I remember saying that if there really was a God, I needed Him to take hold of my life. There was no way I could take on this burden alone. I immediately felt the demons begin to subside and slowly go away. I lifted my head and begged God to help me...and then it happened. I felt a stillness and a presence in my heart that I can't even begin to explain. Suddenly, I knew I wasn't alone anymore. It was as if God put His arms around me and told me that my dad leaving me wasn't my fault. I could feel His hands touch my face, as peace began to overtake my flesh. Benjamin...I knew that I had a friend, a friend that would always be there in good times and bad. The redness in my eyes began to clear up because this color was only temporary. The blue eyes that God gave me were His gift, and they were permanent. The pain that was inflicted on me that day was something I will never forget, but God told me that I can overcome everything through Him. On my 12th birthday, I lost my dad. He would never come back, and there isn't a day that goes by that I don't miss him. But on that same day, I found my Father...and He is still here with me today.

Benjamin began to wipe his tears away, as he put his arms around his Gram. "Gram...can I meet your Father someday?" he asked. "Benjamin, you can meet Him today." And with that, Grace went over to her mantle and reached for her Bible...together, they read John 3:16. When Benjamin was finished, he knew that his Gram was a special gift, and that he would always remember this day as his best ever. His life, just like Gracie's, would never be the same.

The following year, Grace fell asleep on a warm August night...and went to be with her Father. The pain she had suffered was only outweighed by the spirit that lived within her. Just like many of us, Grace was at her lowest point when she found her true Father...but from that moment on, she knew she would never be alone. And the peace of God, which surpasses all understanding, lived in her heart forever. Her eternal Father had picked her up when she needed Him the most. There would be another day, many years from now, when she and her little Benjamin would be together once again.

Pathway of Encouragement

This is going to be a rough year for a lot of families once again, due to the difficult times many have gone through recently. Regardless of one's personal situation, there is no way any of us can get through it alone. God is always here for us...He will find a way to help us get through our own personal challenges. Through our faith in Him, we will find a way to persevere and experience the gift He has given all of us...the gift of grace. For as it reads in James 4:6, "God opposes the proud but gives grace to the humble."

Life is full of painful hurdles, and no matter how old we are, these obstacles never go away. However, our ability to tackle them head-on, with God on our side, is the key. So, how are we able to accomplish this? First of all, we need to partner with God…just like Gracie did. Second, we need to turn to Him for His guidance and strength. He needs to be our best friend because He is the only one who will never let us down. Just like Gracie, many kids have come home to "empty houses" with mom or dad gone, never to be seen again. How in the world is anyone going to get through something like this alone? The answer is painfully simple… there is absolutely no way a child can get through this alone. Let me rephrase this statement…there is absolutely no way anyone can get through this alone. This is why we need to have our constant friend and companion with us at all times. We need to have a relationship with Him first, before we can have a relationship with anyone else. Why? Because He will always be there for us, especially when we need Him the most. And just like Gracie, our greatest day ever will be the day when we turn to Him and accept Him as our true Savior…something that can never be taken away!

Chapter Six

"Best Friends Forever"

Courage...Deuteronomy 31:6

"Be strong and courageous. Do not be afraid or terrified because of them, for the Lord your God goes with you; he will never leave you nor forsake you."

Jack could feel the warm sun begin to peak through the curtains, as he slowly made his way to the foot of the bed. He waited to get his bearings, as it seemed more and more difficult each and every day to get up and tackle the challenges that lie ahead. He began to walk over to the pictures that hung on the wall next to his dresser. Starting from left to right, Jack gazed over the pictures as if he had never seen them before. The family he had raised...the one that meant everything to him for so many years, seemed to come to life right in front of him once again. His beautiful wife, Annette, made the pictures seem perfect. Oh, how Jack loved his wife; she was his dream girl from the day he first laid eyes on her. As he made his way across the wall, his two little "heroes" began to consume most of the pictures. Slowly, they made their way from the toddler years through adolescence, and on to adulthood. Jessica and Jenny were the "apple of their father's eye"...they were such beautiful girls. Jack's eyes slowly began to tear up, as he reached out and touched the final picture on the right side of the wall... the one with his three girls standing together and holding on to each other once again. Their smiles were so beautiful, as they seemed to jump off the page and into his heart like so many times before. The picture was taken 20 years ago to this day, but it seemed like it was just yesterday. This was going to be a very tough day for Jack. He was ready to tackle the world...but just like the past 20 years, he was all by himself with nothing but memories. Jack's purpose for living was one he questioned daily...after all, he had very few friends, and he spent nearly every meal alone. What if I just went away, he thought. Nobody would even notice. Maybe today would be the day...

Brandon lay under the brush, as he slowly watched the shoes walk by in front of him next to the trail. There were five sets of them; therefore, he knew he was outnumbered once again. This had been going on for weeks now, ever since he and his family moved to the Ridgeland, Arizona, area. Brandon had left his closest friends back in Idaho. Even though Brandon was a little slow and wasn't quite as smart as the rest of the kids back home, they were always good to him and were never mean to him. His new school in Ridgeland wasn't turning out to be the one his parents had described when they packed up and left the security of the only neighborhood he had ever known. From the very first day he entered the school, he had been targeted by the roughest group of seventh graders in all of Ridgeland Middle School. They called themselves the "Enforcers", as they seemed to take all matters of the school into their own hands. Over the years, they had been especially cruel to any of the new kids that came to their school. Since Brandon was the only new seventh grader this year, the "Enforcers" had their sights set on him from day one. He didn't stand a chance. The fact that he was a little slower than the other kids in his class made the bulls-eye on his forehead even that much bigger. Every day had turned into a living hell for Brandon. Initially, it started out with pranks like being duct-taped to his locker and having cream pies thrown in his face...events with the sole design of breaking the new boy. Their cruel treatment of him had escalated over the past couple of weeks, and Brandon was beginning to fear for his life. Brandon came to the school with a big heart and an obvious joy for his surroundings, and the "Enforcers" didn't like it one bit. He could tell they were becoming more and more convinced that nobody at the school was going to stand in their way. Brandon was the perfect target, and they knew it. His father traveled a lot, and he was an only child. Nobody was around to stick up for him. Back in Idaho, all the kids got along and they were never in any fights. Brandon was not equipped for his new surroundings, and they knew they were in full control of his life at school. They called him the "Spud"...and they knew he was scared. Who wouldn't be? After all, he was just a good kid from Idaho...

Jack slowly wiped the tears from his eyes, as his mind focused on that last picture. It was as if he had taken it just yesterday. Within one hour from the time he had taken the picture, his life would be changed forever. As much as Jack tried not to digress, he couldn't help but go back to that day...September 15, 1990. He and Annette had planned this trip to the Grand Canyon for quite some time. Since Jessica was getting ready to head off to graduate school and Jenny would be heading back to Cal State Fullerton within the next week for her junior year, Jack and Annette knew the sand in their hourglass was slowly beginning to disappear. They loved to take the girls to the canyon when they were younger, and they wanted to get one more trip in as a family before they were gone. Even though Jessica and Jenny had other interests, they absolutely loved to spend time with their parents. They couldn't think of a better way to end their summer before heading back to school. Jack still remembered the day the picture was taken...the sun was just beginning to peak over the top of the canyon's walls. He snapped the picture and their smiles were perfect...they seemed so alive and full of joy on that perfect day. They made their way back down to the car and slowly began to pull out of the parking lot. Just as Jack was beginning to put the car into drive, he remembered he had set the camera's lens cap on the rock next to the canyon wall. Jack turned to Annette and said, "Honey, I need to run back up to the top of that hill right there. I think I left the lens cap next to where I took the picture. Do you want to come with me, or do you just want to wait here with the girls?" "Oh, go ahead Jack; we'll be just fine," assured Annette. "Just be careful up there and don't fall. We don't want you to get hurt. You are getting older, you know!" And with that, Annette gave Jack the most beautiful smile he had ever seen. He was still so in love with her. He had been so since the first day he laid eyes on her. Jack made his way out of the car and up the hill to the rock where the lens cap still lay. He reached down and put the cap back on his camera, when suddenly he could hear something coming from the distance...he began to hear a loud rumbling noise behind him. As he turned around, he immediately caught sight of the 14-wheeler making the turn just up from the parking lot below him. The truck was going way too fast, and Jack could tell immediately that its brakes must have broken free. Jack felt paralyzed, as he watched the truck heading for his Sedan below. He screamed from the top of his lungs, as he could see it was quickly picking up speed. Jack ran down the hill, but the truck was moving way too fast. Within seconds, the massive truck had engulfed the small car that sat in its path. The sound of that screeching metal would continue to haunt Jack for the rest of his life, as the truck slammed the Sedan into the rocks below. Jack made his way to the wreckage, but there was nothing left. He looked into the pile of metal, and it was as if everything had disappeared. Blood splattered everywhere, and his three beautiful girls were gone. Jack closed his eyes and went into shock, an ongoing trance that consumed his every thought for the next 20 years. If only Jack had not forgotten that lens cap, none of this would have ever happened. His life, his perfect life as he knew it, was gone.

"Where did he go? I know that little punk is around here somewhere. If we catch him today, we are going to make sure this is a day he never forgets." Brandon put his head down and tried to crawl under the brush, as he knew they were getting very close. He did everything he could to hold back his tears. He could feel his heart palpitate, as he lay motionless, hoping that he would not be seen. He was outnumbered once again, and this time there was absolutely nobody within miles to protect him. At least when he was at school, he knew the bullying could only go so far. If they were to find him today, he was afraid he wouldn't get away. He was so scared his face began to break out in a cold sweat, and his whole body began to shake. He could practically reach out and touch the shoes now, as they were right next to him. He could tell by the shoe's unique design on the side that they did, in fact, belong to Tyler Swank, the ring leader of the "Enforcers". Tyler was the one who scared Brandon the most. He had no conscience, and for whatever reason, he absolutely detested everything that Brandon did. He called him the "stupid spud from Idaho"; he seemed to thrive on the fact that he could be so cruel, with absolutely no retaliation whatsoever. Brandon lay his head down on the sand and wished he were invisible, or better yet, he wished he had never been born.

Jack made his way out the front door and down the sidewalk. He needed to get to the market, as he wanted to pick up some groceries for the weekend. Just one bag a week was all he could afford, but oh, how he looked forward to that bag. Today, he was going to take a different route to the store. He never liked to head down by the river, but he knew it would cut at least 20 minutes off his walk, and today he wanted to get back home a little bit earlier than normal. The river made its way through town, and it was very secluded in sections between his house and the store. If Annette was still around, Jack knew she wouldn't approve of him making this trip alone. Just like most of the times when they were together, she would be right once again. His journey was about to begin, but it would be unlike any he had ever taken before. He slowly shuffled down the sidewalk and started down toward the river.

"Oh, look what we have here...our little dumb spud is hiding under this branch thinking we aren't going to find him." Brandon just closed his eyes and waited...he had never been this afraid before. He knew he had been found. With that, Tyler reached down and pulled Brandon out by his hair from under the brush. Brandon just rolled up into a ball, as he felt his body being dragged out on to the trail that ran next to the river. "Come on, guys, we are going to teach this little dumb spud a valuable lesson today. He will learn to respect the "Enforcers" in all that we do. He will bow down to us whenever he sees us, and he will do whatever we tell him. I have an idea…this is going to be fun." Brandon wiped the tears from his eyes, as he felt the rest of the "Enforcers" circle him like a pack of wolves. Five on one…he was in big trouble. "Little spud, I hope you know how to swim real well. We are going to take you down to the river for a swimming lesson and see if a potato really does know how to hold its breath." This was Brandon's greatest fear, as he never learned how to swim as a young boy. He began to shake and screamed, "No, please don't do this to me!", as they dragged him toward the water…

Jack slowly made his way down the hill, as he walked along the trail next to the river. Off in the distance, he could hear the sounds of kids yelling and laughing. Just a bunch of kids having fun on this beautiful day, he thought. As he rounded the corner, he could see that this, unfortunately, was not the case. The group of kids was hovering over what looked like a young boy lying by the bank of the river. They kicked and taunted him, as he held onto the branches that extended from the bank. Brandon's body shook with fear, as the group of teenagers whistled and hollered at him. Jack began to move as fast as he could…he could see the young boy was in real trouble. As he got closer and closer to where Brandon lay, the "Enforcers" turned their attention toward Jack instead. "What do you want, old man? Get on out of here before we teach you a lesson as well. We are just having a little fun with our friend here. We are teaching him how to swim. You see, he is far too old not to know how to swim. Don't you agree, old man?" "Leave him alone," said Jack. "You boys have no right doing this to him. Why don't you get on out of here before you get hurt?" Tyler turned toward his friends and started to laugh. "Fellas, look what we have here. This old man is picking a fight with us. Seems like he has an interest in the spud from Idaho. Let's teach this old man a lesson he will never forget." Brandon felt paralyzed, as he watched his enemies move toward the old man. He wanted to help him, but he couldn't get up enough courage to do anything. "Look what we have here, boys. An old man who thinks he can take all of us," laughed Tyler.

"At first, I really didn't want to hurt this old man, but now I think we need to teach him a valuable lesson for his own good as well. One he will never forget." With that, Tyler reached over and knocked Jack's glasses off his nose. "Ah oh, looks like the old man has lost his little glasses." Tyler threw Jack's glasses to the ground and stepped on them, crushing the frame and shattering the lenses with his foot. The rest of

Shortcut to Heaven

Tyler's henchmen laughed right along with him. Brandon continued to watch from a distance, still doing nothing.

"Come on, fellas, I am not looking for any trouble," pleaded Jack, as he scrambled for his glasses. "Just let the boy go. I am no match for you. I am 80 years old, and there are five of you. I don't want any trouble, please. Just let the boy go, that's all I want." "Well, let me tell you what, old man," said Brandon, as he began to laugh once again. "You just can't get off that easy. You see, we were trying to teach our good friend, Brandon, how to swim. Now, you come down here and decide not to mind your own business, and you have interrupted our lesson. However, you know what, old man. I am a nice guy. I am going to give you the opportunity to take the place of our little friend, the spud. We are going to teach you how to swim. And you know what...we aren't even going to charge you for lessons." Jack slowly backed up toward the river, as the five boys pushed toward him. Tyler led the charge, as Jack began to fall back toward the rocks below.

Back on the river bank, Brandon could feel something churning inside of him. He felt as if his body was beginning to take on a new identity. He slowly made his way to his feet and began to move forward. Tyler lay on top of Jack and proceeded to dunk his head under the water. With every dunk, the rest of the "Enforcers" yelled, "Breathe old man, breathe old man,"…as Jack gasped for his life. "Tyler, get off the old man. I am the one you want." Tyler looked up and there was Brandon, standing over him. Tyler began to get up and turned his attention toward Brandon, as he could feel his blood begin to boil. "You have just made a big mistake. You have called me out, spud boy. I am going to hurt you real bad." "Oh, no you're not. I have had enough of you. Your bullying days are over, once and for all." And with that, Brandon swung as hard as he could…and he caught Tyler right between the eyes! Tyler went crashing back into the bank of the river and lay motionless. The other four enforcers could see in Brandon's eyes that something had changed in him. He was no longer the same kid they had tormented since he arrived from Idaho. Within seconds, they turned and ran down the trail as fast as they could. Brandon walked over to Tyler, as he was still lying unconscious on the ground. Brandon reached down to see if he was ok; suddenly, Tyler opened his eyes and began to sit up. "Tyler, I am going to let you go, but don't let me ever catch you bullying anyone here in school ever again. Do you understand me? If I do, I will personally take this up with you just like I did today. Do I make myself clear?" "I understand, Spud. It won't happen again." Brandon reached down and grabbed Tyler by the scruff of the neck and said, "The name is Brandon. Don't ever call me Spud again. Do I make myself clear?" Tyler shook his head "yes" and began to get up slowly. He started to walk down the trail, holding his forehead. Brandon immediately turned his attention to the old man, as he lay on the bank of the river...

"Sir, are you ok? Please, wake up, sir. Please, wake up. I need you right now. Please, don't go." Jack lay motionless next to the river. His head was bleeding, due to the fall he had just taken. Brandon picked up Jack's head and wrapped his arms around his shoulders. Who was this old man? He came out of nowhere and saved my life, thought Brandon. He was my guardian angel, and he brought out the courage in me that I never knew I had. Oh, please, I cannot lose him now. He is my best friend ever...and I don't even know his name. Jack slowly began to open his eyes, and there he was...his newfound friend. "Hello, son. Are you ok? Are those boys still here, or did you chase them away?" "I chased them away, sir, but if it wasn't for you standing up to them, I would have never had a chance. Now, please, just rest sir; I need to get you some help."

"I don't think that will be necessary, son. You see, for a very long time, my life has had no purpose. I lost my family 20 years ago today and now God has brought me here with you, and I feel like I have a purpose once again. I have literally been going through the motions since I lost them, and now I have met you. You are a special boy. I can feel it. I want to ask you a favor, ok?" Brandon could feel his eyes begin to tear up, as he held Jack's hands. "Yes, sir, whatever you want." "Son, I want you to know that you are a special person. Don't ever let anyone tell you otherwise. You have a spark in your eyes that will never go away. Today...you brought a spark into my life as well. I am very grateful that I took a different route to the grocery store today. God blessed me on this journey because He knew I would find you. You are going to do amazing things with your life because God has a plan for you. He will always be there for you, just like you were here for me today. You see, I am going to be leaving you today, and I am going to be with Him...and I will see my family once again as well. I miss them very much. You have really saved my life, and it is me who should be thanking you. My name is Jack, and it has been a real honor and privilege to have met you today. Now, please go and do what I know you are capable of doing; you are going to make a huge difference in this world. God told me so." And with that, Jack's eyes closed and Brandon felt his hands release. Brandon began to sob, as he held Jack as tight as he could.

His life would never be the same...and he would never be afraid again.

The years went by, and Brandon went on to become the founder and CEO of one of the most successful non-profit organizations in the entire country. The P-KAAC (Protecting Kids at all Costs) organization was all about the establishment of school programs designed to protect kids against all forms of intimidation and threat. These programs focused on building self-esteem in every kid, with the intent of creating a safe learning environment for all...regardless of race or ethnic background. The success of the organization had touched so many kids, and many had been taken out of situations they could have never gotten out of themselves. Brandon's life had been forever changed by the old man on that warm September day by the river...the best friend a boy could ever have. The old man had tapped into his potential and had "lit a fire" that would touch many lives; he truly was making a difference.

Brandon gazed out his office window, while taking in the sun on this beautiful September day. He could still see the blue eyes look up at him, as he held the old man tight. That wonderful old man had touched Brandon forever...and just like he promised him, Brandon would never forget. "Dad, can we go now?" asked the little boy, as he walked into his father's office. "Sure we can, Jack"...and with that, Brandon ran and picked up his beautiful little boy and squeezed him as tight as he could. Jack was indeed a part of him, and for that, he would be forever grateful.

Pathway of Encouragement

We are not to fear man...period. However, all of us will undoubtedly become fearful at some point in our lives, even though we know this fear does not come from the Lord. Why do we do this? Because we are human, and our humanly bodies continue to routinely manifest inadequacies. Hold on...do not get discouraged. So, how do we overcome these fears? We need to focus on the only answer to this question. It really is a simple concept and one we must never forget. The closer we get to God, the more at peace we become and the less fearful of man we are. Proverbs 9:10 says, "The fear of the Lord is the beginning of wisdom, and knowledge of the Holy One is understanding." Once we are able to truly fear God and not man, we begin to take on the wisdom we need in order to fight the fight as His followers. We must fight through our worldly fears by focusing our minds on the Lord.

Fears can consume our daily lives if we let them. Remember, in order for these fears to consume our actions, we need to let them! Do not relinquish your control over your own personal fears; this is very important. Personal fears are disguised in all shapes and sizes because the enemy knows where we are vulnerable. These worldly fears may come in the form of a boss at work, a teacher at school, family members that continue to bring up perceived inadequacies, past illnesses, and many other factors that create fear. We become paralyzed by our fears and thus find ourselves unable to positively impact those around us. Fear will engulf our confidence if we let it; therefore, it is extremely important for us to focus on God the moment we begin to feel fear set in. Simply put...we need to focus on Scripture that directly addresses the concept of fear. Psalm 33:18 says, "But the eyes of the Lord are on those who fear him, on those whose hope is in his unfailing love." The Lord will watch out for us, and once again, we must trust Him with everything.

Only He can help us overcome our fears. Once we understand that we are not to fear man, it will provide us with the confidence we need in order to overcome the pressure we are under. Remember...the beginning of wisdom starts with fearing God, not man. Once we realize this, we can get through anything this world has in store for us.

Chapter Seven

"Steam from a Grate"

Faith: 2 Corinthians 5:7-9
"We live by faith, not by sight. We are confident, I say, and would prefer to be away from the body and at home with the Lord. So we make it our goal to please him, whether we are at home in the body or away from it."

This was a very good night, John Grey thought, as he reached for the old blanket and slowly pulled it up over his head. He carefully positioned himself so the warmth of the soldered iron made like a brace for his tired, weathered back. The temperature was fast approaching zero degrees, and John knew his fellow transients near Pioneer Square would not fare near as well as he would on this particular evening. John's eyes began to close, as he took one last drink…he simply couldn't imagine going to sleep at night without his pint-sized little friend. Falling asleep was the easy part; fighting off the demons that continually reminded him of a life gone mad was what he hated the most. And on this particular evening, his enemies were working overtime. They knew they had to move fast…after years of deadly persistence, he was finally beginning to fall into their grasp.

John Grey walked into the boardroom, and his presence was immediately felt by all eight members of the Executive Team. Just as he had for the past seven years, John ran Genaco Oil with a confidence and a passion that was unmatched in his industry. He had built Genaco Oil from scratch and had seen his countless hours of hard work help elevate the company into the #3 position in North America. The primary objective on this given day was no different than any other day in the quarter…grow revenue, increase margin, decrease expenses, and ultimately, increase cash flow as well. The formula sounded relatively simple; the execution was very difficult. However, John's ability to break down all tactical elements of the business into clearly defined priorities is what truly made him the difference-maker for Genaco. Not only was he a terrific tactician, John also possessed a strategic vision unmatched by his peers. The only thing more impressive than John's professional resume was his "storybook" life away from the office. His wife, Catherine, truly was the love of his life. They had been married now for almost 15 years. Their two children, Benjamin and Veronica, were 10 and 12 years old and fast approaching their teenage years. Everything in his life was absolutely perfect, and he knew it. However, in a matter of seconds, this would all change.

Catherine gathered the kids and packed their surprise for Daddy. The weather was changing quickly, as the snow began to fall and the ice began to take hold. Catherine knew how much work John put into his board meetings; therefore, she always tried to do something nice for him. Once every quarter, she would pick him up at the office when everything was over and take him out for a special evening. Benjamin and Veronica would join her, and they would always bring him a special gift. Over the years, some of the gifts consisted of the Chicago Bears hat in his office, the sleeve of golf balls from Benjamin's first golf tournament, and Veronica's second grade report card…her first of many with straight A's. Catherine pulled away from the driveway and felt especially excited about the present they had picked out for Daddy this quarter…it was something he had always wanted. The year was coming to an end, and it had been one of the best ever for Genaco Oil. Christmas was only two weeks away; therefore, this made it even more special. The weather was changing very quickly, but Catherine still felt like she just had to get to John and celebrate. She knew how much this would mean to him...

As they made the turn just below Cobb Hill, the truck seemed to come out of nowhere. Without any advanced warning, the young man had lost control. Catherine's minivan was T-boned, and the impact was direct. Within seconds, flames engulfed the inside of the vehicle, and everything was gone. The young man was immediately thrown from his truck. He lay helplessly in the snow, as he watched the fire reach up into the sky. Tears began to stream down his face, as he lay motionless on the ground. No cuts or scrapes on the outside, but significant vertebrae damage on the inside. James Stone wished for a moment that he was in the minivan as well, as he wanted to pull himself into the flames. His legs dangled like soft spaghetti, as he rolled over and waited for help. He reached down and grabbed the small package that had somehow made its way through the fire. He put it into his pocket and closed his eyes. He wished it was a dream...but it wasn't. Sirens began to draw near, and James found himself frozen in time. There was nothing anyone could do now...the damage was already done. He began to cry, but nobody was there to wipe the tears away. The evening seemed to go on forever, and his heart began to crack like the fire on a cold winter's night.

John was summoned from the boardroom and was told of the accident that had just taken place. He fell down on his knees and buried his head in his hands, hoping the news wasn't true...but it was. In a matter of seconds, his beautiful family was gone, and he had nobody. He was all alone...his body was already beginning to feel numb with sadness and inexplicable pain. It would be the last time he ever set foot in the Genaco Oil Building...nothing seemed to matter to him anymore. His extended leave of absence was put in place, but everyone was convinced it would be permanent. In fact, nobody had any idea where John decided to go. He sold their house and everything in it. He cashed out the family's investments and made one final contribution to Children's Hospital...all in the name of an anonymous donor. His desire was to get rid of the family memories, drift away, and unceremoniously take his own life as well. Somehow, he felt this sequence of events would get him back to his family once again. For years, the plan was in John's mind, and now it was just a matter of following through with the final event. Maybe this would be the night, John thought, as he rolled up into the fetal position under his blanket. John could sense something was about to happen...he felt different on this particular night, for whatever reason.

His face was unrecognizable now, as five years of living on the streets will do that to a guy. John didn't blame anyone for his life of destitute; he just didn't want anything to do with anyone right now. His three best friends were gone, and his sole reason for existence had been taken away. Maybe this would be the night that would provide him with the peace that he was so desperately searching for. The demons wanted to get rid of John now, as they knew his heart was still special. The sooner, the better. They knew he had the gift of moving people in a positive way, and they didn't like it one bit. They played with his mind and found his weakness on a continual basis. "Why weren't you with them? You knew about the bad weather, yet you chose to do nothing. You have always been more concerned about your career than your family. Admit it! Well, look at you now, hotshot. You have neither! Ha, ha, ha..." John pulled the covers over his head and slowly screamed his way to sleep. "Go away... please, go away!" he shouted. But they didn't. They giggled in unison, as they knew they were starting to get to him. It was his mind they wanted...because they knew that once the mind collapsed, everything else would go with it as well.

James Stone was now 24 years old and had been confined to a wheelchair since the accident. His evenings were filled with nightmares; however, James had an incredible persistence that would bring him closer and closer to John since the crash. The night of the accident would torment both of them for the rest of their lives; James knew he needed to find John in order to clear his own head and move forward. On this faithful night, James felt like something was, in fact, different. He had an old picture of John that he found in the local paper shortly after the accident, and he kept it with him at all times...but what would this man look like today? James pulled himself out of his vehicle and strapped his legs into his chair. He began to move toward the group of men who had gathered just ahead. James took the picture out of his pocket and passed it out to the men hovering around the fire in Cheeseman Park. This was a favorite place for the transients to gather, and James had been there many times before. However, tonight was beginning to feel much different. James began to ask the men a lot of questions, just like all the other evenings. One of the men signaled to James and said, "Yes, I've seen this guy before. He hangs out down by the pier near that old grate by the water. He thinks he owns the place. He isn't very friendly, and he doesn't smoke either. In fact, I think the man is downright rude! When you see him, can you do me a favor? Tell him to jump off that old pier and get out of our lives. We don't need his sorts around here. In fact, maybe we all ought to just go down there and take care of him ourselves." With that, the group of seven chuckled and passed the bottle of whiskey around the horn. James nodded and proceeded to push himself down the steep hill toward the water. He could feel in his heart that he was getting close. What on earth was he going to say? He had to move quickly...he knew that he would soon have visitors.

John could feel the warmth of the grate below him, and for an instant, he remembered the electric blanket that he and Catherine used to joke about so often. Like so many couples, she was warm-blooded and he was cold. She used to kid him; she told him that he never hugged her in bed anymore. John would respond by saying that it wasn't her; it was just that her side of the bed was always 10 degrees warmer than his, due to the electric blanket. Then, she would laugh and set her control at a "7"...and his would be set at low. Oh, how he wished he was at a "7" right now...

James slowly approached the dark figure huddled next to the grate, and he just knew this was it. His heart began to race, and he took a deep breath. Perspiration settled above his top lip, as he slowly pushed himself closer and closer. He was now right next to the dark figure; however, he could see no face. He reached down and gently tapped on the body, but there was no movement. "Sir, sir, wake up, please. Please, turn around; I am here to help you." Was the man dead, or was this even the person James so desperately needed to find? He had come to realize that his life would remain in neutral until he released the guilt that had consumed him since that tragic night. Or was that even possible? There was absolutely no movement. "John Grey, is that you? Please, I need to speak with you. My name is James Stone. You probably have no idea who I am, but I need to talk to you." James underestimated the mind of John Grey, and his memory as well. Although his physical appearance had shriveled up on the outside, his intellect was still far greater than that of an average man...even after all the self-inflicted damage he had done to himself.

John rolled over and there he was...James stood there motionless and in shock. John shook his head three times, as he tried to make the young man go away. This was not a dream...his "demons were finally coming to life", John thought. He tried to speak, but nothing came out. Silence crept up on the two of them like the shadow of the sun, as it maneuvers its way across the sky on a bright sunny day. This was the day that both of them had dreaded but needed just the same. "Hello John. I am James Stone. I have never met you, but I am,"…he couldn't finish the sentence. What was he going to say? "I am the man who killed your family,"…or, "I am the one who ruined your life,"…or, better yet…"I am the reason you spend your evenings on this old grate, hoping for steam to keep you warm." James dropped his head into his hands and began to weep uncontrollably. The echoes from his cry seemed to cut through the pier at 67th Street like a sharp knife. John watched this man with compassion, as tears began to slowly trickle down his face as well. John reached out his hand and squeezed James's left forearm. It had been five years since that dreadful night, and both men could feel the other's undeniable pain. It was the first time, since the accident, that both of them were not alone.

John whispered to James, "I forgive you, now please leave me alone, so I can die in peace." James began to speak and John simply squeezed his hand a little harder and whispered once again, "Please." James nodded his head and knew it was time for him to leave. He needed John's forgiveness, and it was delivered…through the only source that had the power to do so on that dark night. John began to pull away and slowly made his way back toward the grate. James wasn't through; he had one more thing to say. "I have something for you, John. It was next to me at the accident, and I knew I had to find you and get it to you. Somehow, through everything, it made its way to me. My only regret is that it has taken me so long to find you. Here you go." Out came the small package that had been in his possession since the crash. The bow was still neatly tied, and the light blue wrapping paper was surprisingly still in tact. On the white card were the words, "Daddy, we love you." Small little signatures engulfed the corners of the card. Catherine, Benjamin, Veronica...John began to cry like a small child, as he stared at the box. James put his head down and closed his eyes. He would never forget that painful sound...and the stillness that surrounded both of them.

John began to unwrap his gift. He slowly folded the wrapping paper and placed it into his coat pocket. He took the card away from his chest, kissed it, and held it with all the strength he could garner. He would never let it go. The box was now exposed, and he began to open the lid. His hands were shaking so badly, that suddenly, the box fell from his grasp. It was like slow motion, as both men watched it float through mid-air, heading right for the grate. There was no way they would retrieve the box if it fell in, and they knew it. However, the box miraculously landed directly on the middle pipe and seemed to spring off to the side, without entry. It came to rest just outside the last pipe, as John quickly reached down and picked it up. Inside the grate, the demons protracted back into their resting place. They knew, at least this time around, they had been defeated.

John opened the box, and there it was…a note from his three best friends in the world, the only friends he really knew. Catherine, Benjamin, and Veronica had each taken turns with the words that made up their final message to the man that meant everything to them.

It read:

"Dear Daddy, this is our most special gift ever. We hope your new buddy is our buddy too! We love you, and we are so proud of you."

Love,
Daddy's Angels

John turned the card over and it read "Redeem for puppy of your choice at Bogaard's Puppy Palace". John looked at James and shook his head in disbelief. James read the card and knew this was his only chance to save John. "I am taking you there, John. Right now, I am taking you over there. Through new advances that have been made, I am able to drive my car…and I have never known of a better reason than this to take advantage of the gift I have been given.

You need to come with me." "I can't go," whispered John. "I just can't do it." James felt an incredible, sudden burst of confidence, and he began to reach out and pull John into his chair. "I am not letting you go, John! Please, let me take you to Bogaard's. I live about three blocks from there. I will drop you off, and you never have to see me again. Please, let me take you." John was way too tired to say no, as he stood up with the box in his hand. "Let me at least push you," said John. And with that, John turned the chair around and began to roll James back up the hill.

On that special December night, a bond was created that would never be broken. James would devote the next six months of his life to one thing…cleaning up his newly found friend. In addition, John would try to give back as best he knew how; through the positive gift he had been given. He would devote the next 12 years of his life to the creation of the largest Spine and Neck Rehabilitation Center on the West Coast. The Greystone Rehab Center would become world famous, not only for the tremendous patient care they gave, but for their sincere compassion as well. Everyone knew the care that was given truly came from the heart…one that had slowly been mended over the years.

As John settled into his desk, he stared across the room, as his eyes honed in on the mantle just above his fireplace.

From left to right, there were his most precious memories. The Chicago Bears hat, the sleeve of Benjamin's first tournament golf balls, and Veronica's second grade report card; right next to his most sacred memento of them all... the little white box with the handwritten card. John reached down below and slowly caressed the only companion he had known for the past 12 years. Somehow, some way, John had found peace through that dog and finally made it through the storm. Ben had become much more than a pet to John...he had become the most important figure in John's life. As he looked into Ben's eyes, he could see the family he once had, and he knew they would be very proud of him today. John whispered to Ben, as he pulled the big golden lab up onto his lap, "I love you boy, I really do." All Ben could do was wag his big old tail, which for John, was more than enough. Finally, through all the pain and suffering, John Grey could feel himself smile once again.

Pathway of Encouragement

John Grey represents a little bit in all of us...fear, compassion, perseverance, strength, and most of all...faith. The pitches come one by one, but through continual resolve, we seem to foul them off in search of the perfect strike. Although that pitch may never come, we seem to settle in with singles and possibly a double or two along the way. As we grow older, we realize that life is a winding path and nothing can break a person's will to survive and move on…unless he or she allows this to happen. The mind is the gateway to the soul; therefore, we must always keep our thoughts sharp and focused on Him. A few drops of the chin, but at the end of the day, he or she has made it through the journey…and we must keep our head held high. All of us can definitely relate to John. We never believe that the man sleeping on the grate could, in fact, be one of us. We walk quickly by the transients in our own home town and hope they stay on the other side of the street. Their eyes are never seen because we refuse to look into them. The tears that swell simply evaporate and are never wiped away by another…because there is no other. Some tears freeze, while others simply drop to the ground like a leaf in the forest, but we all stay away from that forest because ours is warm and safe. At least for now…

All of us hope we never, ever become the next John Grey. However, why does it take a wake-up call like this story to get us to act? It shouldn't…in fact, all of us should try to reach out and truly make a difference simply because it is the right thing to do. You don't have to go to Skid Row or Cheeseman Park to find loneliness…just take a look next door or in the aisle next to you in church...or in the school...or at the crosswalk. Loneliness is everywhere. Maybe all of us can find a way to reach out and positively impact the next John Grey. A smile, a nod, or better yet, a warm hello may be all it takes to help push that person up the hill a little further. Every push really does get us closer to what we all long for...true peace in our heart. Not an easy thing to accomplish and impossible to do alone. We all need that little push, whether we admit it or not. The bathroom mirror continues to slap all of us in the face routinely, as life flies by at record pace. We cannot slow it down, as our attempts are futile. However, we can take a deep breath and enjoy the days that have been given to us. Easier said than done, but living for the day is really the key. Today has to be the first day of the rest of our lives...each day is a new beginning for us, one where we have an opportunity to truly make a difference. Let's be sure not to let it slip by... for once it is gone, we cannot get it back.

How many of us have walked by a homeless person and immediately said to ourselves, "Wow, I'm sure glad that isn't me,"...or, "How in the world does someone end up like that person and just basically give up on his or her life?" In the same breath, we also think to ourselves that there is no way I will ever let that happen to me. However, many of these individuals are just like John Grey. Something has happened in their lives that has basically caused them to give up. We have no idea what this "trigger" may have been…it could have been alcohol, drugs, a divorce, a bad accident, or the loss of a loved one or an entire family, as in John's case. We tend to have the same feeling when we visit a friend or a loved one at a nursing home. Once again, we begin to rationalize as to what may have caused this particular individual to be in such a depressing place. We vow to never, ever let this happen to us…but, once again, we have no idea what is in store for us. Many folks in a nursing home had little or no say regarding how they got there. Some have had strokes, some have fallen and broken a hip, and others have fallen prey to diseases like Alzheimer's or Dementia. Regardless of whatever the circumstance may be, nearly everyone who sleeps on either a park bench or in a nursing home bed never thought they would ever end up there. For most of these individuals, this will undoubtedly be the last stop. We know it, and so do they! What a depressing thought…so, what can we do? Just like James Stone in "Steam from a Grate", we cannot continually turn our backs on these individuals and hope the problem will mysteriously go away.

In Proverbs 28:11, it is stated that, "A rich man may be wise in his own eyes, but a poor man who has discernment sees through him." Wow! This is the perfect verse that reflects the condition that most of these folks are in. Just think...most of these people know they have been shunned by society, and they know that everyone wants them to just die and simply go away. Can you imagine going through life this way? People who sometimes seem like they are oblivious to their surroundings may, in fact, be one smile, handshake, or a small hug away from getting back on their feet once again. The next time you find yourself avoiding these individuals, remember that most of these people were just like you and me at one point in their lives. A few bad breaks here or there, and everything is quickly turned upside down. Through our own faith, we can make these people stronger, and we can help them believe once again. Please, don't ever pass a steel grate without remembering John Grey...I am sure there are others just like him if you look close enough.

Chapter Eight

"Til Death Do Us Part"

Peace: 2 Corinthians 13:11
"Finally, brothers, good-by. Aim for perfection, listen to my appeal, be of one mind, live in peace. And the God of love and peace will be with you."

"**P**apa, we're going to be late for the movie. You know how much we like to get candy before it starts. Hurry up, Papa. Please, hurry up!" Little Sarah loved her grandpa so much and going to the movies was her favorite thing to do. Papa would always take her to their favorite candy store before the movie started, and she would go through every single jar in the shop. That was the fun part... for both of them! Each time she was there, Sarah seemed to end up back at her favorite jar...she just loved those Snocaps.

However, the looking and wishing part was when she was the happiest. Just her and her Papa, he was her favorite...

"Sarah, your Papa wants to look perfect just for you, so he is in his room getting himself real handsome right now. You are his number one girl, you know," smiled Nana. "I know, Nana. Do you really think I am his number one girl right now? If I am, then why did he marry you?" Nana laughed at her five-year-old granddaughter...she always wanted to know why. However, this time she would be saved by the entrance of her own prince charming...George "Papa" Joseph, her best friend and devoted husband for the past 57 years. "I see you, Papa, there you are! Let's hurry up and go to the movies," screamed Sarah. George looked over at Rose and said, "So, how do I look, honey?" Rose shook her head and said, "You look very handsome, George." Then, Rose glanced down at George's feet and noticed he was wearing two different shoes. She slowly led him back into the bedroom and sat him down at the end of the bed. "Let's change your shoes, honey. I think these ones here will go better with your pants." Rose took George's shoes off and replaced them with a pair that matched. George just smiled and said, "I really love you, sweetheart. You are always so good to me." Rose looked at her George and slowly turned her head away to hide the tears that began to form in her tired eyes.

Her George was starting to fade away right in front of her. Rose knew this would more than likely be the last time Papa would be able to take his little Sarah to the movie alone...

At the tender age of 17, George Joseph truly was a "man among boys". He had been swimming competitively for the past 10 years, as he had worked himself into prime condition. Grandview High School was always one of the top high schools in the state of Indiana; however, they had never seen anyone there quite like George Joseph. His nickname at the school was "The Porpoise", and that suited Rose Louise Waters just fine. "So, how does it feel to be dating a porpoise?" teased her friends. "It feels great," responded Rose Louise, "after all, he is the best looking porpoise I have ever seen!" With that, all her friends would just laugh. They all knew deep down inside that George and Rose were meant for each other. George went on to win all four events that year at the state championship, and Rose was there to cheer him on at every stop along the way. George and Rose decided to get married the following year, and life had been perfect for her ever since. George was a man of integrity and honesty, and they went on to raise two beautiful daughters together. Everything was just how Rose had dreamed...until now. Her heart was slowly beginning to break...

"Here you go, George," said Rose, as she helped him get his pajamas on later that evening. "Let's go back into the bathroom and get you ready for bed." George reached out for Rose's hand, as he shuffled his way toward the bathroom. They slowly walked arm-in-arm, just like on their wedding day, as they made their way across the room. Finally, they made it to the bathroom. Rose began to wash George's face and then carefully brushed his teeth. Over the past six months, she had painfully watched her George go from a man of total independence to a boy with a mind of a three-year-old. Rapid Dementia had set in, and now he was unable to do anything on his own. Rose continued to smile and slowly combed George's hair. "You have beautiful hair, George...does this feel good, honey?" George looked at Rose's beautiful eyes, smiled, and said, "That feels very good, Mommy." Rose set the comb down on the edge of the sink and responded, "You need to get your rest tonight, Georgie. Let's get you to bed." "Thank you, Mommy, I love you," said George. "I love you too, Georgie," whispered Rose, as she moved him over to the bed. Rose reached over and pulled the covers back, as it was time to call it a day. She tucked George into bed and slowly began to rub his eyebrows. Her best friend in the world was no longer there. Rose slowly began to cry, as she found herself terrified of what was yet to come. George had told her a long time ago that he never, ever wanted to be put in "one of those old folks homes that smelled real bad". This had always been George's worst nightmare...and Rose knew it. "Take me out of my misery, and yours, if I ever lose my mind," he would say. "Oh, George, I would never be so lucky. You will always be a step ahead of me. You aint goin' nowhere," Rose would laugh. Oh, how she wished that was the case right now. Rose would give anything to have her "hero" back...

Rose began to fall asleep, when suddenly a noise came from the foot of the bed. She reached over and said, "George, there is someone in our room!" She pulled the covers back, but George was gone. Rose moved down to where she heard the noise come from, and there he was. She froze...and found herself staring in disbelief. George lay in the fetal position sucking his thumb, clutching on to one of his favorite blankets. Rose gathered her bearings and gently helped George back into bed. "Are you ok, honey?" asked Rose. With that, George looked at his Rosie and said, "Tonight is the night, sweetheart. I don't want to live like this anymore. You promised me you would never let this happen to me. Please, please keep your promise. Don't you love me? I am not the man I used to be, and I am getting worse. Help me, please. Everyone is laughing at me and pointing fingers...I can feel it. I just want to die." Rose laid George's head on the pillow and made her way out to the hallway. She sat down on the floor and slowly began to cry. She had been holding everything back for a long time now, as her husband seemed to be getting worse by the day. George was right…for many years; they had talked about their fear of nursing homes. Both of them had promised each other that, "No way either of us would ever let that happen." Promises were made but never in a million years did Rose ever think their worst fear would actually play out. What was Rose going to do…she never thought George would be the one who would slip away. He was always so strong. She took a deep breath and went into the kitchen. Her mind began to race. Rose opened the cabinet, and there they were. There had to be at least 100 sleeping pills still left in the bottle. Rose grabbed the bottle and continued to weep, as she made her way back to the bedroom. She leaned down and slowly lifted George's head. She helped him up and rested his head on the pillow next to the headboard. Rose cried harder, as she reached for the glass of water that was still on the nightstand. George slowly opened his eyes and whispered, "Thank you, honey. I will always love you." Rose wiped her tears away, as she poured the bottle of pills into her open hand. She raised the glass to George's lips and began to open his mouth. Suddenly, she heard a tapping on the window of their bedroom. Rose turned around and there he was...the most beautiful white dove she had ever seen. The dove continued to tap harder and harder on the window pane, until Rose finally set the glass of water down and walked over to where it had landed. She opened the window and put her hand out. Instead of flying away, the dove slowly brushed his head along Rose's outstretched hand. For what seemed like an eternity, the dove caressed her skin...and Rose felt total peace. She was afraid no more. Before Rose knew it, the dove was gone, but her heart was calm and still. She went back over to George, who was now fast asleep. She put the lid back on the bottle of pills and lay down next to her best friend once again. It simply wasn't his time...and she knew it. Rose closed her eyes. It had been a very long day.

The sun felt incredibly warm, as it seemed to peak through the curtains and into their room. Rose tapped George on the shoulder and said, "We need to get up, George. Today is a very special day...Sarah will be here soon." The summer had flown by, and now it was their favorite time of year. Not only was September the month that brought beautiful, crisp mornings to Grandview, it was also the month that marked Sarah's birthday. This year was going to be extra special, as Sarah had planned this day for a very long time. Rose felt compelled to have a party this year for Sarah, as she knew George's days at home were numbered. This could be the last chance for George to be with his little girl before he was gone. Rose quickly decorated the downstairs, as George sat in his chair and slowly nodded off. Two hours passed, and then it was time. "Ding dong"…the door bell rang, and there she was. "Nana and Papa, I am here for my party. I have a new dress on that Mommy gave me this morning. Papa, it is your favorite color!" Sarah's mom, Maggie, decided that she would let her mom and dad have little Sarah until 3:00 p.m. that afternoon. Maggie had planned a surprise party at home for Sarah; therefore, this would work out perfectly. She could get all the details together while Mom and Dad watched "their little princess". Everything seemed to be perfect on this day; however, this temporary state of euphoria was all about to change. "Papa, come see me. I am beautiful, Papa, just like you said I was." Rose helped George out of the chair and said, "George, it's Sarah. She is here for her party. Let's go see her." George looked at Rose and slowly shook his head. "Who is Sarah? I don't know anyone by that name," responded George. "She is your granddaughter, George. Your beautiful little girl is here to see us for her birthday." George slowly got out of his chair, reached for

Rose's hand, and said, "Let's go meet Sarah, honey. She sounds very nice."

Rose had done a very good job of hiding Sarah from George's condition; however, this day would reveal challenges like none she had ever seen before. Sarah was her typical self, as she continually asked George questions... but today, there was very little response. The three of them made their way out to the backyard and sat down near the creek bank that flowed through the corner of their property line. Fed primarily by the irrigation controls up north, the creek was unseasonably high on this particular day. Rose sat down, took a deep breath, and gazed at the scene that seemed to captivate her thoughts and recollections of what used to be. Sarah looked absolutely beautiful in her new dress and seemed to be very content, as she lay on the hammock with her chilled glass of lemonade. "Oh, my gosh!" said Rose. "I need to get your cake out of the oven, sweetheart. Can you watch your Papa for me, and I will be right back?" "Sure, Nana," answered Sarah, "I like to take care of my Papa." Rose ran into the kitchen and went straight to the oven. She moved quickly, as she didn't want to leave George for too long...

Sarah looked over at her Papa, as he started to fall asleep on the chair next to her. She was really starting to miss her old Papa...the one that seemed to have left her this summer. He just wasn't the same, she thought. For the first time in her life, she felt sad. It was a "yucky" feeling, she thought, and she didn't like it much at all. Just then, she heard something move over near the water. Sarah had turned, and there he was...the small puppy had fallen into the creek and was hanging on to the branch of the old cedar tree that extended out over the water. Somehow, the little guy had grabbed the branch as it was going by, and now he was hanging on for dear life! Sarah got up out of the hammock and ran over to George. "Wake up, Papa, wake up. That puppy out there needs our help!" George slowly got up out of his chair, as Sarah pulled him closer and closer to the creek bed. The water gushed through the small ravine that bordered the property, and the little black lab was in a clear state of desperation. If he let go of the branch, he would be gone with absolutely no chance of survival. Before George could get his bearings, Sarah had already made her way out on to the branch of the tree. "I'll save him, Papa. He is going to be ok, he needs me right now!" Sarah quickly made her way out to the end of the branch to where the puppy was holding on. She dangled over the raging waters, as her new blue dress seemed to clutch the branch as well. As Sarah reached down to get the puppy, the sound was deafening to George, as he found himself frozen in time. Crack! Down Sarah went into the cold waters below, as George helplessly watched on. "Help me, Papa!" screamed Sarah, as her head began to bob in and out of the whitecaps that had quickly engulfed her.

The scream sent a cold chill into Rose's body, and she knew immediately that something terrible had happened. The cake fell to the kitchen floor, as Rose crashed through the back door. George stood on the bank for a split second, as Rose shouted, "No, George, don't jump in!" It had been nearly 60 years since his days at Grandview High, but on this particular day, he felt like his old self once again. His thoughts were focused on one thing…and that was saving his little girl. George dove into the water and quickly reached out for Sarah's hand. The water was swift, as it pulled both of them under the tree at the bend in the creek. George embraced Sarah and did everything he could to keep her head above water. On this blessed day, George's mind and body were sent back in time. He quickly made his way to the shoreline and propped Sarah up on the side of the bank. He reached into her little mouth, pressed his lips close to hers, and slowly began to breathe life back into her little body. He gave her everything he had, as Rose made her way down the side of the bank to where the two of them were lying. Sarah started to cough, as water shot out of her little nose.

Rose reached down and wrapped her arms around her cold little body, "Please, don't leave us, Sarah. We need you." Sarah slowly opened her eyes and whispered to Rose, "Is my Papa ok?" Rose looked over, as George had somehow crawled back over to the embankment. She gently placed Sarah's head down on a patch of grass and made her way over to George. His back was facing Rose, as he seemed to be clutching on to something under the sleeve of his torn shirt. Rose reached over and could hear the gentle whimpers of the little black lab. She turned George's body toward her, as her eyes began to tear. The rocks from the creek bed had pierced his head during the struggle, and his scars were still fresh. He was hurt real bad. "Oh, George! Please, stay with me. You can't leave me now. Please, please stay." Slowly, George's eyes began to open and a smile took hold of his weathered face. "Today is the day I go, Rosie, but I promise I will be waiting for you when you get there. I love you,"… and with that, George's eyes began to close, and his body exhaled his final breath. George was right…this was indeed the way he would have wanted it, for he was a champion at Grandview High once again.

Sarah made her way to the bend in the creek, until she was back to the spot where her life was changed forever. There it was; the same place where she had gone every Sunday for the past 10 years. This was the one place where Sarah felt total peace. "He was a very special man, simply the best. He was my Papa," Sarah whispered. The wind slowly blew through the green pasture, as the two of them stood there in silence. Sarah looked down at her buddy and slowly rubbed the back of his neck. "Let's go home, Georgie." Sarah reached down and gave her best friend a kiss on the cheek. He had been there through it all, and the two of them would be forever linked on that September day. Georgie wagged his tail and brushed up against Sarah's leg. Papa had saved both of them on that faithful day, and they were here because of what he had done. Somehow, through it all, God had found a way to save Papa as well. God was, in fact, the true hero once again.

Pathway of Encouragement

The world we live in is changing right before our eyes. At times, many in this world simply don't want to go on, and everything seems to be a big waste of time. This is where we as God's people need to be strong, as we must stay focused and help those that are in need. God knows how much we can handle, and He will never take us past our limitations…no matter how difficult things may be. Just like George Joseph in this story, God wasn't going to let him quit…He sent His dove to Rose to remind her just how beautiful life really is. Rose was ready to take George's life; thank God she didn't. For if she did, Sarah would have been gone as well. When things look hopeless, we all need to hang in there and persevere...we cannot quit! This is where we all grow and earn our stripes as followers of God. He has a plan for all of us, and He already knows the outcome. Working within His time parameters is the toughest thing for us to do because we all want it to be fixed today. We must believe that He will protect us and never forsake us. If we do have this divine faith, we will always see things in a positive light, and the enemy will be defeated once again.

As the mind of our loved ones begins to fade away, we see them mentally digress right in front of our eyes. Watching our parents or loved ones lose their faculties is one of the most difficult things we will ever go through. I have seen firsthand the pain that is caused when individuals are faced with difficult decisions as to whether or not their loved ones should be admitted into a nursing home. None of us want this to happen to us; however, it is never that simple. Factors weigh into the decision that cannot be planned for, and families can be literally torn apart during the process. I have no idea what the right answers are, but once again we need to trust God, because He is in control. There is a bigger picture that He sees and we don't...and we must trust Him, even when we feel the pain of watching a loved one fade away. I have a grandmother now who just turned 102! Every time I visit her, I am convinced it will be her last day. The last time I traveled to see her, I told my daughter before I left that I was sorry I had to leave, but, "I just didn't know how long Gram was going to be around." With that, my daughter responded, "Daddy, I don't want this to sound bad or anything, but we have been saying that for a real long time!" You know...she was definitely right! However, the will to live is incredible. How many times do we hear others say, "I just don't want to live that long," as they reference someone who may be in their 80's or 90's...or maybe even 100! You know...until that person is "us", there is no way we can accurately make that statement. Chances are, every one of us will want to continue to go on if we get to that age. No matter what age we are, it always seems younger than it did 20 or 30 years ago! Just like Rose did in "Till Death Do Us Part", we need to take care of the ones we love, no matter how old they are. Who knows...someday, that person who needs help may be one of us.

Our greatest concern for those we love is we must be able to honestly answer the question, "Where are they going when they die?" We need to be at peace with the answer to this question...we need to know, without a doubt, that our loved ones are going to heaven. We cannot wait until the last minute to try and save those we love...we need to reach out to them today! Our greatest gift to those we truly love is to tell them about Jesus and how He died for our sins...and how He is our answer to peace. In fact, He is the only answer to true peace...no matter what age we are.

Chapter Nine

"The Blue Ribbon Prize"

Thankfulness: Colossians 3:17
"And whatever you do, whether in word or deed, do it all in the name of the Lord Jesus, giving thanks to God the Father through him."

The man found himself leaving the office in the dark once again, many hours after the end of the day. The trunk opened and in went the briefcase. It was almost as if this day was simply a repeat of many before, as he slowly made his way to the driver's seat. He took a deep breath and turned on the ignition. He began to pull out of the parking lot and found himself drifting back into the events of the day. Why did he feel so frustrated when those around him seemed to be unfazed by the recent lack of productivity in his company? Although the drive home was close to 45 minutes long, the thoughts that consumed him night after night always seemed to make the trip go by much faster. His mind raced, as he methodically replayed the discussions that somehow came to life as he lost focus on the drive once again. His mind never seemed to slow down…it only picked up steam as the darkness set in. This had always been a problem for him…

He swerved in and out of traffic and soon made his way back home. He turned into the driveway and slowly pulled into the garage. The door closed behind him, as he shut off the engine. The man sat and listened to the stillness around him and seemed to sigh in desperation, as he reflected on the day that was now behind him. Oh, how he needed to tell someone what he was going through…there was only one person who truly understood. He lifted his chin and slowly rubbed his eyes with both hands. He began to get out of the car and slowly made his way to the door leading into the house. The house felt empty, as his family was in bed once again. His best friend would hopefully be waiting for him…

The door slowly began to open, and she could see the shadow of his figure make its way toward the bed. She rubbed the sleep out of her eyes and softly whispered, "Honey, is that you?" The man was hoping she was awake, as he quickly replied, "Hi, honey, I just got home from the office. I hope you are not asleep. I really need to talk with you tonight." Without hesitation, the woman sat up and turned on the light next to the bed. "What is it?" she asked, as she slowly began to gather up her senses. This was the invitation he was looking for. "You are not going to believe what is going on at work right now. These days keep getting more and more difficult, and nobody there seems to care about winning or losing anymore. Not only do we have a great chance of finally reaching our objective, but I really think our window of opportunity will soon close if we are not careful. Every night, I do all I can to get out of that office on time…and it never seems to happen." The man continued to unload on his wife, trying to describe the events that led up to this late night barrage. His wife seemed to hang on every word and simply shook her head in agreement. Where appropriate, she interjected words of encouragement that seemed to make it all feel better to him. This is what he loved about his wife…the 30 minutes he spent with her late at night was not only therapeutic, but it seemed to recharge his batteries for another day. This cycle went on continuously, and every night, his wife was there to answer the bell…never complaining, and never unresponsive. In typical fashion, the man would slowly get ready for bed and turn to his wife for her reinforcement. Although there were numerous times when she felt like pushing back, she simply smiled and said,

"I agree, honey…you are definitely doing the right thing." She knew in her heart that this was what he needed to hear. And just before finally turning off the light, he would seem to reserve the last 30 seconds of the discussion to see how her day went. Each night, she would answer him the same way. "Everything went well today, dear, not a whole lot to tell. The kids and I had another uneventful day, but a great one nonetheless." With that, he would roll over and for the first time all day, he would feel at peace. The man was finally at home where he belonged, as he felt like everything he had done that day was somehow worthwhile. He found himself begin to drift off, and soon he could feel himself start to fall into a deep sleep. However, this night would be different…

The clock moved closer toward the 2:00 a.m. hour, and the man could feel himself start to shake. He was in a deep sleep; however, he was now moving from a catatonic state to one of subconsciousness. His dream was about ready to intensify, and he could actually feel his body start to anticipate his next move in the warm confines of his own bed. His dream was officially underway; however, this one would be much different than anything he had ever been through before…

The man found himself in his car making another trip to the grocery store, a relatively harmless dream that seemed

Shortcut to Heaven

to have very little meaning at the time. As he pulled into the parking lot, he caught a glimpse of a young woman entering through the front door. He could not see her face, but oh, how she captivated him so. He quickly shut off the car and proceeded to run after her. She went in the front door and slowly disappeared around the far left aisle of the store. The man had no idea who this woman was…but he felt like he simply had to find out. As he began to walk around the end of the shelf that encompassed the aisle, he heard a crash. The man peeked around the corner and saw the woman helping up an older lady who had just fallen next to her shopping cart. Rather than reaching out to help her, for some reason, he just stood there in amazement, as the younger woman held her fragile body and slowly caressed her damaged brow. "Are you ok, ma'am…we seem to have collided. I am so sorry." With that, the older woman began to cry and slowly wept in the young woman's arms. "I am so grateful you are here with me. I just lost my husband, and I can't seem to get him out of my mind. I was daydreaming and just didn't see you here. I am so sorry." The younger woman said nothing and reached out to embrace her once again. With that, the older woman reached into her purse and said, "Here, I want you to have this…it was given to me by my late husband, and I really feel like I need to pass it on. You have been so nice to me…I insist you have it." With that, the older woman reached into the younger woman's hands and placed into them a small, blue ribbon. The younger woman smiled and said, "A blue ribbon...what does this mean?" The older woman slowly began to sob once again and said, "My husband always said that I was his blue ribbon prize...number one in his heart. I want you to know that today; you are number one in my heart as well." Before the younger woman knew it, the older woman was back on her feet...and she was gone.

The man felt compelled to continue following this younger woman, as she made her way to the produce section of the store. He wanted to see who she was; however, her face was just outside his view. Just as he was ready to get close enough to capture her attention, he immediately heard the argument that was taking place just on the other side of her cart. The screaming voices caught the attention of nearly everyone in the store and before anyone could react, the woman he was following was wedged between the man and woman who were fighting. Her innate ability to quiet down the couple left the man in awe, as he stood approximately 30 feet from where the incident took place. Within minutes, the argument was over, and the woman was back pushing her cart once again. As she maneuvered her way around the cereal section, she grabbed a couple of boxes of granola and made her way to the express line. The man was still unable to see her face; however, he did catch a glimpse of the burgundy wind-breaker she was wearing. Oh, that jacket looked so familiar...he had seen it before, but he could not remember where. If only she would turn her face; he could finally put this mystery to rest and get some sleep. The woman began to push her way out the front door, as she immediately moved toward the older gentleman who was shaking the donation bell in front of the store. She began to converse with him, and she gave him a small contribution. The old man smiled and watched her move toward her car in the parking lot. Although the contribution was similar to others he had received throughout the day, it was the way she gave that felt different to him. Her heart was pure and her spirit humble. He could feel it...

By now, the man was practically running out of the store in search of this mystery woman. He absolutely had to meet her, as he made his way to the stall where she had parked her car. She slowly began to put the car into gear. The man reached out and grabbed the handle of the door, but it was locked. With that, he began to pound on the window, and almost in slow motion, the woman began to turn her face toward him. Just as her face was coming into focus, the man began to shake uncontrollably. His eyes opened, and he found himself staring at the ceiling. He felt his shirt, and it was soaked. Unfortunately, his dream had come to an abrupt end without his approval. He reached over to make sure his wife was ok. The man felt his heart begin to settle down, as he caressed her long, black hair with his fingertips. Finally, he was back in bed where he belonged.

He felt at peace and went back to sleep. Within what seemed like only a minute, the alarm clock went off, and the man was about to begin another day. He made his way to the shower and began to think about the dream he had just had. Never before had he dreamt about another woman... who was she? In a way, he felt guilty about his dream, as the woman had captivated his every movement. There was really nothing for him to feel guilty about, because after all, it was only a dream...but oh, what a woman she was! The man turned off the water and made his way to the master closet. He entered the doorway and immediately felt the presence of something, or someone, behind him. He slowly began to turn around and suddenly became fixated on the article of clothing that lay in the corner of the room. The man slowly fell to his knees and began to weep uncontrollably. The sounds of his voice resonated throughout the house, but nobody came to see what was happening. He finally found the strength to pull himself up and began to crawl toward the garment. His sobbing intensified, as he slowly reached out to the dark piece of clothing. There it was...the burgundy windbreaker from his dream. Folded perfectly on the floor next to his wife's small dresser, it seemed to call out for him to embrace it. The man reached out and buried his face into the side of the coat, immediately smelling the warm fragrance of his beautiful wife. He reached into the pocket of the burgundy jacket, and there it was. He closed his eyes, lifted his hands in praise, and slowly began to cry out to the Lord, "Never again will I take anything for granted. My life is no longer about me, but instead, it is about you dear Jesus." With that, he took the little, blue ribbon out of the pocket and gently rubbed it against his lips. He knew that God had used this dream to send him a powerful message. He walked over to the bed and reached out and touched his wife. He leaned over and kissed her, and told her he was sorry. "I love you, honey...thanks for saving me," he said. And in slow motion fashion, one of his tears fell and landed on her brow. "You are welcome," she whispered. She proceeded to close her eyes, looked toward the sky, and smiled...for in the end, it was, in fact, her dream that had now come true.

Pathway of Encouragement

All of us are guilty of not recognizing what God has done for us, how He has brought so many wonderful, loving people into our lives. Work consumes our daily thoughts, as we continually regurgitate on the events of the day with those around us...then, we get up and start all over again. We go to the well in hopes of finding something there...something we can tap into for strength once again. Why do we continually need wake-up calls in order to recognize the important things in life? I have been extremely guilty of unloading on my wife every night for a very long time...rehashing the events of the day on a continual basis, practically begging for her approval. And like so many faithful spouses out there, she always agrees with me regarding every single issue we discuss. I know there are times when she thinks I am wrong, but she approves of my actions anyway. I need to be a better listener and take a vested interest in her day as well. By showing true empathy for her day and the challenges she has been through, I will become a better husband and far better father in my daily life. In "The Blue Ribbon Prize", we see where it takes a life-changing dream to actually trigger the thoughts of recognizing a loved one...in this case, his wife. The best thing we can do when we are going through difficult times is reach out and give thanks to those individuals who stick by us, regardless of the challenges we face. True friends are the ones who continually support us in all we do, not just during the good times, but the bad as well. Being thankful should not be contingent upon the situation we are in; it should be a way of life. And...the first one we should thank every day needs to be God. Whenever we wake up, it is a good day! Now, we need to go out and show Him just how thankful we truly are...not just through words, but by our actions as well.

Just like the man in this story, many of us have been saved through the daily actions of the ones we love. Many of us take these actions for granted. Had it not been for this love from those around us, we would have never found the true peace we have been granted. Our lives would have been nothing more than a dead-end street. We have been given the greatest gift of all...everlasting life. We can never take this gift for granted; we need to reach out and thank the one responsible for this precious gift. More than likely, he or she is right there in front of you today. Please reward him or her with a "blue ribbon prize" for a job well done...you have been saved. How wonderful is that!

Chapter Ten

"My Last Day"

Love: John 3:16-17
"For God so loved the world that he gave his one and only Son, that whoever believes in him shall not perish but have eternal life. For God did not send his Son into the world to condemn the world, but to save the world through him."

Her hand reached out and began to pull his sleeve toward the bed. With what little strength that was left, Emma felt a strong desire to pull her true love just a little bit closer. He leaned down and whispered to her, "I love you...I have always loved you." He felt her grip loosen and could see in her eyes that her fight was about to end. Her beautiful, blue eyes were still the color of the sky on a crystal, clear day...and her face reflected that childlike glow that drew him close to her nearly 60 years ago to this day. Her breathing seemed to be moving in slow motion today, as her life was getting close to the end. Oh, how he wanted to go first. The thought of living one day without her was more than he could bear to imagine. But somehow, Stan knew that he had to be strong for his dear Emma. He began to rub her eyebrows and Emma's eyes started to close. As Stan gazed down at his one and only true love, his mind drifted back to that first day he saw her. Oh, what a sight she was…one that he would never, ever forget. His smile began to form, as he laid his head next to hers on the pillow. The smell of her skin wrapped around his neck like a cold, satin pillow case, and soon his dreams felt like they were coming true once again. He felt at home with his Emma…his love and his life.

The clock ticked down to zero, as Morton Grove had just accomplished the "unthinkable". This 1930 season had ended with a perfect 22-0 record, and that elusive state championship trophy was finally theirs to keep. This was the first of its kind for the Morton Grove Mustangs, and everyone in attendance felt like it represented a piece of them as well. Basketball was, in fact, a way of life in this small Indiana town; however, nobody in their right mind ever thought this could possibly happen. Morton Grove had just defeated the mighty Westchester Maroons for the trophy they had coveted for the past 17 years. Stan Voorhees, the hometown prodigy, calmly sank two free throws with just four seconds remaining to secure the win...and now he was the toast of the town. The young man could run for mayor and probably get elected on this memorable night, as the game of basketball was somehow able to elevate this small town from the bowels of the Great Depression...at least for a day. The clock seemed to be moving in slow motion, as Stan reached up to cut the nets from the rim. Cheers pulsated his ears, as he could hear his teammates chant, "Stan-ley, Stan-ley, Stan-ley!" As he turned his eyes back toward the crowd, it was as if the moment he had dreamed of was about to come to an abrupt stop. Stan slowly turned his head to the side, as he soon became focused on that one event that would change his life forever...an event he wasn't prepared for. His eyes became frozen in time, as the small, dark figure slowly moved to the corner of the gym. There she was...the most beautiful thing he had ever seen. Her face turned toward Stan and slowly her smile began to consume his every movement. Those eyes...those big, beautiful, blue eyes. Suddenly, cutting down the nets and hoisting the trophy seemed irrelevant.

Stan slowly felt his eyes begin to open. His greatest fear seemed to be only a heartbeat away. He whispered, "Wake up, Emma...I am here to take care of you." There was no answer. "Honey, it's time to get up. We have lots to do today." No answer again. Stan could feel his heart begin to race, as he reached over and gently began to rub her arm. "Please, wake up, honey...please. I need you." For the first time in his life, Stan Voorhees was all alone. Tears began to roll down the side of his face, as Stan nestled his face next to Emma's. His whimpers began to call out for help... yet no one was listening. It felt dark...and cold...as Stan pulled the pillow over his face. His whimpers soon turned into screams, but just like the sounds from before, they fell on deaf ears. Emma's blue eyes were closed, and Stan knew in his heart they would never open again.

Two years had passed, as Stan still felt the pain of Emma's loss control his every breath. Joining her would have been so much easier, but for some reason, his health seemed to be stuck in neutral. No better, no worse. Nothing in his life had any purpose, and even he couldn't "die the right way". Every night his prayers would focus on one thing...and that was his hope for one final breath. Praying to God and asking Him to take him away went against everything he stood for, but now that Emma was gone; his purpose for existence was dead. His body was alive, but his soul was beginning to decay. He didn't like himself much anymore. Life's daily routine was nothing more than a cup of coffee in the morning, a cup of soup for lunch, and the nightly news for dinner. Every day...the same ritual. No friends, no family, no fun. But... as he reached over to pull himself out of bed, Stan Voorhees decided that this day would be different. This day would be his last.

Stan closed the door behind him, as he left for Danny's Bakery at a quarter past nine. This was his usual time, but on this day, Stan decided that he would finally change his ways. After all, it was going to be his last day and a cup of coffee seemed so inappropriate. Not just *a* cup of coffee...this last breakfast had to be special. "Hello, Dorothy, how are you today?" "I am doing great, Stan, and how are you?" Dorothy knew the padded answer was about to come her way once again, just like it had for the last two years. She could feel herself sarcastically mumble under her breath ..."not too good today, Dorothy, but I guess it's better than the alternative, I think." The same answer had been recited for far too long, but Dorothy seemed to need it every day. But on this day, much to her surprise, the answer would be different. "I am great today, Dorothy. Today is a perfect day to live... or to die. Either way, I win." Dorothy began to laugh and looked back at Stan to see what had gotten into him. Her anticipation suddenly turned to dismay. For the first time ever, Stan's face looked completely lifeless. Something was wrong with him today, and for the first time, Dorothy felt as if death had entered the building. She felt cold and scared, as she turned to go back to the kitchen. "Stan wants an omelet today, Eddie...make it a good one." Eddie reached for the eggs and cracked them wide open. He looked up to make sure the order was right. "I'll make sure it's a good one, all right." And with that, Eddie threw in a little extra cheese just for good measure.

Stan wiped his chin and took a deep breath. He could not remember ever having a breakfast taste so good...and when was the last time he even had an omelet? He knew it was long before Emma died, as his daily routine of "coffee and nothing else" had started shortly after her passing. "How was the omelet today, Stan?" asked Dorothy, as she reached over to fill up his cup once again. "It was wonderful, Dorothy...a great way to start the day. Oh, and Dorothy...I just want to say "thanks" for being so nice to me since Emma's passing. You've always been there to listen, no matter how busy you are. Through everything, you have found a way to ease my pain, and I will be forever grateful. You are a very special lady, and I really do appreciate all you have done for me...I wish you nothing but the best." Dorothy began to laugh and replied, "Oh, Stanley, enough of that. You talk like you are planning to go somewhere. I will see you again tomorrow, and I will do the same thing I always do. And you...you will probably start ordering omelets from me every day and really make me work for my money!" As Dorothy glanced down at Stan, her heart began to sink and her body felt numb. Fear consumed her, as she felt a chill slowly creep up the back of her neck. Here it was once again...that awful feeling that only the pain of death can create. Just like she did when her mother passed away years ago, Dorothy felt paralyzed with nothing to say. She could see the pain in Stan's eyes and, at that moment, she knew that his pain was far greater than she ever imagined. "I will see you again tomorrow, right Stan?" Stan's smile slowly formed but seemed to stop midstream. He had thought of this day for quite some time...and his eyes began to blur. He turned away and quickly rubbed away the tears that were forming. As Stan slowly walked toward the door, Dorothy wished he would turn back around and reassure her that everything was ok. However, she realized it wasn't...and she knew this could very well be the last time she would ever see him again.

Stan slowly walked up to his porch and sat down in the swinging chair. It just never felt quite the same since Emma left, as this was where they would spend their summer evenings rehashing the activities of the day. Emma was always such a good listener and always seemed to make Stan feel better. No matter how bad the day was, he would somehow put everything behind him for his Emma. The silence since her death was one of the most difficult things he had ever had to deal with....the quiet nights continually exerted a pain that just wouldn't go away. Stan sat back in the chair and thought for a moment. "What do I have to live for?" he asked himself. He had no children, no wife, no job, and very few friends. The weather on this particular day was absolutely spectacular, and the breeze felt perfect on his tired face. He had thought about this day for a very long time now, and he felt like everything was coming together just how he had planned. He had just finished "the perfect breakfast" and now his day was being blessed with a feeling of absolute closure. Stan reached for his glass of lemonade and savored every last drop. He took a deep breath and began to move toward the front door of his house. This was where he wanted to be...to do what he felt had to be done.

Reaching for the bottle that sat on the middle shelf of his cabinet, Stan could feel his left hand begin to shake. He began to unscrew the lid and slowly started to take the pills out of the bottle, one by one. The bottle was almost full... probably close to at least a hundred pills, he thought. On restless nights, he knew how tired just one pill had made him...surely, he had plenty that would now accomplish his goal. Stan reached into the refrigerator and slowly began to take the cold bottle of water out for his final drink. He filled his glass and moved slowly toward his favorite chair that sat in the corner of the living room. This was always "his chair", and now it would be his final resting place. "Take the drink, old man," whispered the dark, raspy voice. "You are a nobody...and now it is time for you to shut your eyes forever." The voice had started to torment Stan in his dreams many months ago, yet he was able to fight it off time and time again. Tonight, he felt as if he was powerless. The voice consumed him...it tormented him...and now he was starting to believe the words himself. Stan turned the bottle over and began to pour the pills into his open hand. He looked at the glass and closed his eyes. "Drink it, Drink it...you are a loser." The voice pushed and pushed...and Stan put the glass to his lips...and began to close his eyes.

"Bam, Bam, Bam"...the front door sounded like it was going to cave in. Stan waited to see if the noise would go away...after all, he had one final job to do and now he was being interrupted. He waited and hoped the sound would stop so he could press forward. "Bam, Bam, Bam"...he thought the door was going to crack. What in the world was going on? Stan immediately sat up and placed the glass of water on the table next to where he was sitting. He opened his hand and rolled the pills out on the table as well. "Forget it, Stan, finish the job, you loser. You are a quitter...finish the job...finish the job," chanted the voice. Stan shook his head and made his way to the front door. He opened the door and there she was...how something so little could make such a big noise was beyond comprehension. The little girl looked up at Stan and screamed, "I need your help, sir. We live down around the corner, and I can't find anyone around here today. My daddy is hurt real bad. He needs your help, or he is going to die. Nobody else is around today and your house is the third one I have knocked on. Please, help us...please, come quickly!" Without thinking twice, Stan found himself running after the little girl. They made their way around the corner, as she headed straight for the second house on the left. "My daddy is trapped down in the basement and is in a lot of pain," cried the little girl. Stan followed her in the front door and went straight for the basement stairs. He could hear the man downstairs screaming...and soon he got down to where he was lying. Stan looked around for a flashlight and saw one sitting over on the work bench. As he brought the light closer to the man, he could see why the little girl was so hysterical. He was in bad shape and needed to get help right away. "Go up and call 9-1-1...and then get me a long string or even a shoelace. We are going to get your daddy all better, but I am going to need your help." He looked into the man's eyes and said, "You need to keep your eyes open and stay with me. I need you to stay with me...and whatever you do, do not go to sleep."

The little girl came running down the stairs and soon made it to a spot next to Stan. "I made the call, mister...and they said they would be here right away. Is my daddy going to die? Is he going to leave me just like my mommy did? Please, make him stop crying...make him stop screaming." Stan reached down and could sense the man was starting to drift off. His leg had been crushed by the old, steel beam, and he had already lost a lot of blood. Stan knew it was dangerous to move him, but he had to stop the bleeding or the man wouldn't make it much longer. "Did you get me the string?" asked Stan, as he began to assess the man's leg. "Here you go, sir...I took the lace out of my shoe. Is this going to help you?" Stan nodded his head and immediately tied the lace just above where the damage had occurred. He tied it as tight as he could...and squeezed with all his strength. He had to get the knot to hold and then hope that help would arrive soon. There was no way the man would make it much longer. His body was starting to feel cold, as he had lost a tremendous amount of blood. The little girl leaned over and put her head on Stan's shoulder. "I can't lose my daddy," she said. "He is all I have." Stan could feel her pain...and he closed his eyes and began to pray.

Down came the three men, as they quickly reached the scene of the accident. Within minutes, the beam was lifted off the man's leg, and the oxygen tank was running at full throttle. They hooked him up to an intravenous and quickly began to administer three pints of well-needed blood. Stan could sense they were well-versed on these types of accidents, as they quickly had things under control. They strapped him onto the stretcher and moved their way up the staircase within seconds. Stan reached out and held the little girl's hand, as they followed her father out the door. "We need to take your son to the hospital," said the lead paramedic. "We think he is going to be ok, but we need to get him stabilized, so we can stop the bleeding once and for all. You saved his life...another 30 minutes, and he would have bled to death. Why don't you and your granddaughter follow us down to Evergreen Hospital, and then we can get all his personal information. We really need to get him in now. Thanks again...you and your little girl make a heck of a team." Stan was speechless. He didn't know what to say. Everything had happened so quickly that he didn't have time to do anything. The paramedics thought his son was the victim, that the little girl was his granddaughter, and that he was now going to take her to the hospital. Granddaughter… during all the chaos, he wasn't even able to get her name. The ambulance door shut and soon it was speeding off in the distance. Stan and the little girl watched it take off, as it seemed to move at record pace. Just then, Stan felt the little hand reach up and tug on his shirt sleeve. He knelt down and, for the first time since she banged on the door, he felt connected to the little girl and gazed into her beautiful, blue eyes. He could feel his heart begin to race uncontrollably. The little girl stared at Stan, and everything seemed to freeze in time. "You can be my grandpa, sir…I don't have one, and I would love to have you as mine. Will you, sir…will you be my grandpa?" Stan stared into her eyes and felt his knees begin to buckle. "I would love to be your grandpa…but first, I need to know your name." "My name is Emily…but my daddy calls me Emma. I like Emma better." And with that, Stan knew he had found his Emma once again. "Emma it is then," Stan said. "Now…let's go take care of your daddy." Stan reached down and held his little granddaughter's hand as tight as he could. Emma had come back…and once again, he was made whole.

Pathway of Encouragement

I want each of you to think about the one person who means more to you than anything in this world...now close your eyes and try to capture the pain you would feel if that person was on a cross, battered and bloody, dying an unimaginable death right in front of your eyes. His or her sides pierced and face nearly unrecognizable due to the brutal beating that just took place. And to think that this person did this for us...so that we wouldn't have to! It is impossible for any of us to even begin to go down this path, but it is important for us to somehow get this picture in our minds, as we continually struggle with the true priorities in our own personal lives. How can we possibly quantify the love that God had for us when He gave up His one and only son...for each and every one of us? This was the ultimate act of love that we must never lose sight of in our daily walk. Our lives on earth have been made possible through Him, and our love for those around us has only been made possible through His love for us. In the story "My Last Day", Stan illustrates the incredible human love that one can feel for another here on earth. Stan's life totally revolved around his wife, Emma, and when she was gone, he did not want to go on. This happens to many of us here on earth when we lose that one person who has made our life whole. However, as difficult as it may be, we need to somehow look at the big picture and realize that once again, God is in absolute control of everything. We need to turn to Him in order to get through the pain, but we also need to realize that there is a bigger picture and that _only_ He sees it. Our minds are tactical, He is strategic. We will be with our loved ones again in heaven...we need to truly believe this in order to go on each and every day. However, we also need to stay focused on Him in all that we do. While we are here on earth, we need to touch those around us who need our love and support...in everything we do.

Kids have a way of bringing out the love in all of us. Look at little Emily in this story...better known as Emma. She reached out and grabbed on to Stan's heart and made him realize that it was ok to miss his Emma. This is something we need to embrace because it is normal. However, we also need to realize that God is in control and our work here on earth is never over, until we are called to be with Him. We have no idea when this calling will take place; therefore, we need to live each and every day as if it was our last. We hear this all the time, but it really is the mindset we should have on our journey. The pain we feel when we lose a loved one is natural, and God knows more than any of us just how riveting that pain can be. Now, here comes the hard part... we must find a way to go on. We must find our calling and passionately go after it with all our heart and soul...with absolutely all of our personal strength. Although Stan was planning out his own personal death, it was not his place to make this determination. Again...everything we do in our life needs to be on His schedule, not ours. Someday, we will know why things happen like they do. In His time, everything will make sense and Stan will be back with his Emma, right by God's side where he belongs.

<u>Closing Remarks</u>

Sense of Urgency: Psalm 37:5
"Commit your way to the Lord; trust in him and he will do this: He will make your righteousness shine like the dawn, the justice of your cause like the noonday sun."

Our strong desire to band together as brothers and sisters in Christ will provide us with the perseverance to go on and fight the good fight; to ultimately win the battle. For the battleground is before us; therefore, we must rise above the obstacles that surround us in order to persevere and, in the end, claim victory. We must firmly believe in our heart of hearts that God is in full control of our lives and that He, in fact, does see the big picture. Although we may be going through difficult times right now, we must keep our heads up and our eyes focused on the prize...because the prize is wonderful. It is within our grasp...we just need to reach out and get it. Everlasting life is available for each and every one of us to attain...what an incredible gift we have been given!

So what is the shortcut to heaven?

John 3:16-17...“For God so loved the world that he gave his one and only Son, that whoever believes in him shall not perish but have eternal life. For God did not send his Son into the world to condemn the world, but to save the world through him.”

Romans 10:9...“That if you confess with your mouth, “Jesus is Lord,” and believe in your heart that God raised him from the dead, you will be saved.”

All you need to do today is pray these Scriptures above with all your heart, ask God to forgive your sins, and accept Jesus as your Savior...it really is that simple! This is the shortcut to heaven that every one of us must take; we need to come together as brothers and sisters in Christ because this world needs us. The path to heaven is lined with believers who will help each of you reach eternal peace, something that nobody can ever take away! You have made an incredible step forward…one you will never regret. And just like Grace found out in the story "Eyes of Blue", this will be your best day ever too!

Shortcut to Heaven has given me a renewed passion for what God has in store for all of us. The road to heaven may be bumpy at times, but we must continue to help each other as we encounter challenges along the way. I hope and pray that each of you find the words in this book to have true meaning in your life. I am truly humbled by the opportunity God has given me to share these inspirational stories with you, and I am grateful for the outpouring support we have already received…this book could not have been possible without your prayers and incredible encouragement.

God Bless you always…see you in heaven!

Robert Bush

Breinigsville, PA USA
07 April 2011
259379BV00001B/1/P